WILD + FREE HOLIDAYS

35 Festive Family Activities to Make the Season Bright

AINSLEY
ARMENT

Pepparkakor recipe on page 36 used by permission of Gwen Welk Workman of The Wooden Spoon, Plano, Texas.

HarperCollins books may be purchased for educational, business, or sales promotional use. For information, please email the Special Markets Department at SPsales@harpercollins.com.

FIRST EDITION

Designed by Janet Evans-Scanlon

Library of Congress Cataloging-in-Publication Data has been applied for.

ISBN 978-0-06-299818-7

20 21 22 23 24 LSC 10 9 8 7 6 5 4 3 2 1

WILD + FREE
HOLIDAYS

"Winter is the time for comfort,
for good food and warmth,
for the touch of a friendly hand
and for a talk beside the fire:
it is the time for home."

—EDITH SITWELL

CONTENTS

Come Home for the Holidays by Ainsley Arment ix

Pumpkin-Beeswax Harvest Candles
by Leah Damon 1

Fall Felt Leaf Crown
by Naomi Ovando 4

Pumpkin Cottage
by Elle Celaya 8

Mother Earth Wool Felting
by Katrien Van Deuren 11

The Thankful Tree
by Lea Wu 19

Mothers as Memory Makers
by Rachel Kovac 22

Finding the Perfect Tree
by Chelsea Holland 25

A Picture Book Christmas
by Alisha Miller 28

A Celebration of Light
by Amanda Gregg 32

Winter Table Piece
by Katrien Van Deuren 38

Natural Christmas Tree
by Rachel Kovac 42

Turning Artwork into Festive Decor
by Heidi Eitreim 48

Collecting Ornaments
by Kirsty Larmour 53

Hand-Embroidered Star
by Lea Wu 54

How to Draw a Christmas Wreath
by Kristin Rogers 59

Wool-Felted Advent Spiral
by Leah Damon 62

Christmas Garland
by Carol Ann Sartell 67

A Mother's Search for Light
by Leah Boden 70

Snowflake Art
by Kristin Rogers   72

Arroz con Leche
by Cynthia Garcia   77

Nature-Stamped Ornaments
by Naomi Ovando   79

Christmas Cookies as Handcrafts
by Sharon McKeeman   84

Book Advent
by Jamie Wolma   88

Holiday Crowns
by Suzi Kern   90

Mistletoe Kissing Ball
by Lea Wu   93

Homemade Advent Calendar
by Kristin Rogers   96

Handmade Wrapping Paper
by Hannah Mayo   99

The Lion, the Witch,
and the Wardrobe
by Hannah Westbeld   102

Storybook Ornaments
by Carol Ann Sartell   104

Rustic Woven Winter Stars
by Leah Damon   107

Paper Stars
by Rachel Kovac   113

The Promise of a New Year
by Ainsley Arment   120

Midwinter Lanterns
by Katrien Van Deuren   122

Mindful Love Baskets
by Leah Damon   128

Wildflower Valentines
by Nichole Holze   133

Cupid's Arrow Valentines
by Shannon Mooers   138

Royal Icing Cookies
by Erika Yung   141

The Spread Love Project
by Jillian Ragsdale   144

Resources and Materials   149

Contributors   151

About Wild + Free   159

Credits   161

COME HOME FOR THE HOLIDAYS

Each fall, I lament the darker days and colder nights. Yet by the time December comes around, my heart settles into the home in an absorbing, contemplative, and satisfying way. Somehow, as the world embraces us a little more tightly, I feel it breathing new life into our rhythms, rather than suffocating them.

While the world rushes about doing, going, buying, and bustling, we slow down and embrace the home more than ever before. We make the most of what this time of year can offer in the ways of learning, crafting, reading, gifting, and eating.

We embrace the state of being housebound due to winter's chill and make the most of our togetherness indoors. We focus more on caring for each other, nurturing our sibling and family relationships, and cherishing our favorite holiday traditions.

This involves a lot of handcrafting, baking, and reading our favorite festive stories. It's starting a fire and piling all the blankets and pillows on the floor for a day of reading, board games, and snuggling. Some days, it looks like baking gingerbread or decorating sugar cookies until it's dark outside and time to make dinner. And sometimes it's letting everyone do their own thing, including Mama.

But most of all, it's meeting my kids where they are because I can't expect them to be interested in what I want to do if I haven't invested in their worlds. This is a yearlong goal of ours, but this time of year really beckons us to slow our pace and rediscover the joy of being together.

Home isn't four walls but the relationships within them.

Friends, as we enter a season when the world calls us to clutter our calendars, fill our refrigerators, and empty our pocketbooks, the home beckons us to rest. Be still. Revel in simple. And savor our moments.

In these pages, you'll find ideas for slowing down and enjoying time with your kids around the winter holidays. From handcrafts and family recipes, to decorating trees and reading festive books, you'll find some wonderful traditions to enjoy with your family this year.

I've included a variety of projects, so look for the icon next to each that indicates whether the project is better for beginners (easy enough for young children to do with minimal help and supervision), intermediate (some adult participation and supervision needed), or advanced (will need adult participation and supervision).

Beginner

Intermediate

Advanced

I've also included a resource section on page 149 that will direct you toward a suggested list of items to keep in your supply cabinet so that you're well-stocked to do these projects.

My hope is that we will listen to our hearts and respond with thoughtful action. That we will look our children in the eyes and know that this time together is what matters most. May our homes burn bold and bright this season. And may our hearts rest in the glow of our children's eyes reflecting the love they feel from us.

AINSLEY ARMENT
Editor

Katrina softly touched the drawing board. She wanted to say, *How wise and wonderful you are, Papa* and *Thank you, Papa* and *I'll always love you, Papa.* But all she could say was, "Oh, Papa."

Papa didn't say anything either. He just handed her the three sticks of charcoal.

PUMPKIN-BEESWAX HARVEST CANDLES

As we focus our hearts on this seasonal time of gratitude for the Earth's simple gifts, my children and I have been doing the academic work of studying seed types, gardens, soil, the process of decay, and the cyclical rhythms of planting and harvesting.

While we gathered the little gourds, beeswax, and supplies for this harvest craft, I had many conversations with my son Shiloh, the littlest in our family, about the seeds he would find inside his mini pumpkin. But it wasn't until I cut off the stem and he reached inside for *himself* that he exclaimed, "Mom! Guess what! I found seeds inside here!"

It was a meaningful reminder of how valuable it can be to bring tactile, hands-on learning into our homes. We can read or describe many beautiful and worthy things to our children, but feeling, tasting, smelling, or experiencing learning in some form of intimate sensory relationship offers the opportunity for deeper understanding.

I love that the home invites flexibility and freedom for this type of learning. It is a beautiful thing to watch children welcome life and learning into their own hands, to roll their learning around, to smell it, to squeeze it between their fingers, and dig ever deeper into the wonder that learning about the world around them can be.

This craft is a fun way to turn our fall pumpkins into works of art that give off a cozy glow as the days grow shorter and cooler.

MATERIALS

Mini pumpkins, gourds, squashes
Beeswax (block or pellets)
Wooden wicks with metal bases
Sharp knife
Spoon or melon baller
Scissors
Microwave-safe glass measuring cup (I keep a dish in our art room that I use solely for melting beeswax or you could use a double boiler)
Thick towel or hot pad
Star anise
Cinnamon stick

 **SAFETY TIP**

Sharp knives, scissors, and hot wax can be dangerous and should be used with adult supervision.

INSTRUCTIONS

1. Cut off the top stem-portion of your pumpkin or squash with a sharp knife to expose the seeds within. (This is certainly a job for an adult or older child, since many gourds or squashes take a fair amount of controlled strength to cut through the rind.) You could alternately cut a small hole in the side of a larger horizontal squash that will lie sturdily on its side, if you wanted to leave the stem intact. Be creative with whatever quirky shapes of harvest produce are available in your area at this time of year.

2. Use a spoon or melon baller to scoop and scrape out the seeds and "guts" of the pumpkin. Be sure to adequately scrape the bottom of the inside to ensure there is a nice flat surface for the wick base to rest on when it comes time to pour your wax.

3. Once you have removed as much of the inner goop as you can, insert a wooden wick into its metal base and position the base in the bottom center of the hollow pumpkin. Use your scissors to trim the wick to the appropriate size (slightly above the pumpkin's top).

4. Carefully melt your beeswax. If you are using the microwave method, place beeswax in a glass cup and be sure to microwave in short increments and stir occasionally as it melts. Once it has melted completely, use a towel or hot pad to gently remove the dish, being careful around little fingers, as melted wax is very hot.

5. Slowly pour the melted beeswax into the hollow of your pumpkin until it reaches the top of the carved pumpkin rim. Gently tap the sides of the pumpkin to bring any potential air bubbles to the top. If the wick moves a little from its original position, grab the exposed portion of the wick and tease it gently back into a centered position while the wax is still in a liquid state.

6. Position a few pieces of fragrant star anise or cinnamon stick on the surface of the hot wax. Allow the candle to cool and set overnight before burning for the first time, then enjoy the lovely harvest glow.

BY LEAH DAMON

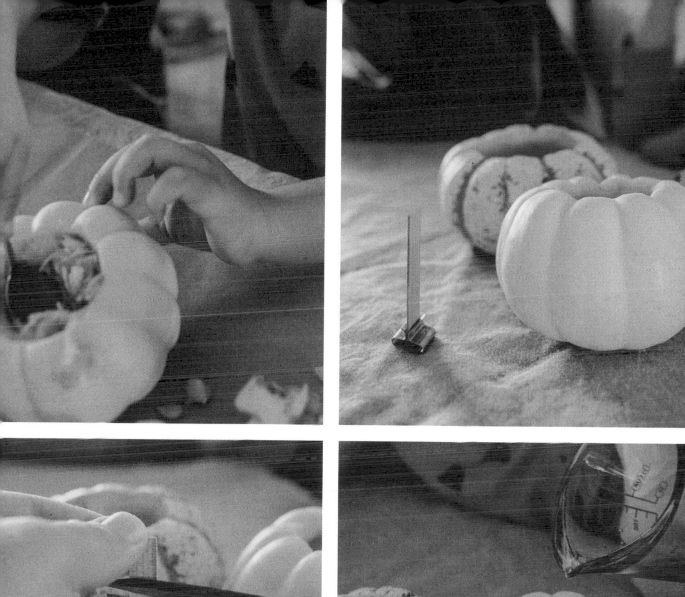

FALL FELT LEAF CROWN

This season is filled with golden sunsets, crisp air, and leaves in a palette of beautiful reds, oranges, browns, and golds. I intend to leave margin in our days to notice the beauty around us and to bring it into our home.

One way my family does this is by making nature-inspired fall felt leaf crowns. Every time I look at them, it reminds me of the beauty outdoors. Here are the steps to make your own.

MATERIALS

Wool felt sheets in autumn colors

Leaves or leaf shapes

Scissors

Low-temp glue gun or another type of glue

Embroidery thread

Large-eye needle

Wide ribbon or elastic

SAFETY TIP

Hot glue and scissors can be dangerous and should be used with adult supervision.

INSTRUCTIONS

1. Gather leaves or cut out leaf shapes and use them to trace leaves onto the wool felt sheets. Cut out desired number of leaves for your crown. (I used approximately fourteen leaves for our crown.)

2. Use your embroidery thread and needle to add details, such as leaf veins, to your leaves. A sewing machine can also be used for this step.

3. Lay your ribbon or elastic flat on the tabletop. Take your leaves and begin to arrange them on top of your ribbon. Once you are happy with the arrangement, glue them down with your hot glue gun or other type of glue.

4. Let the glue on your leaves dry, then join and glue the ends of the ribbon together to make a wreath the size you want. After the glue is dry, enjoy wearing your fall leaf crown!

BY NAOMI OVANDO

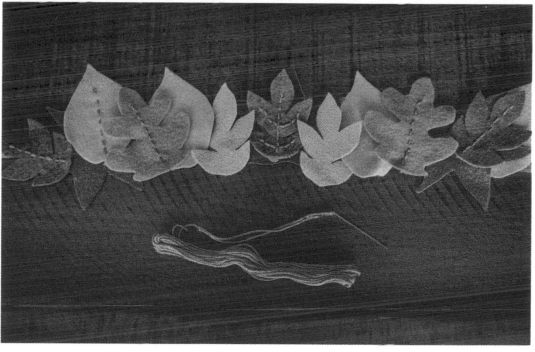

PUMPKIN COTTAGE

From the first colored leaf to the Thanksgiving feast finale, fall brings an extra measure of coziness and gratitude into our homes. Celebrating seasonal traditions old and new is one of my favorite ways of bringing my family together throughout the year.

This year we started a new autumnal tradition of carving a pumpkin cottage, a fun twist on the usual jack-o'-lantern. My kids loved helping out with the process, and they especially loved playing with the pumpkin home for hours after it was built.

Crafting a pumpkin cottage is an activity your entire family will enjoy, and the finished cottage is sure to bring autumnal charm into your home the moment it is illuminated.

MATERIALS

Medium pumpkin

Spoon

Carving knife

Hot glue gun

Pencil or pen

Nature finds such as pinecones, twigs, dried flowers, leaves, stones, wood slices, and moss

Wooden peg dolls or other loved figurines

Candle or LED light

 SAFETY TIP

Hot glue and carving knives can be dangerous and should be used with adult supervision.

INSTRUCTIONS

1. Using the carving knife, carefully cut a hole at the top of the pumpkin around the stem as you would for a classic jack-o'-lantern.

2. Use the spoon to scoop out pumpkin pulp and seeds, making sure to scrape a flat area to set your candle.

3. Using a pencil or pen, sketch where you will cut out the door and windows (rectangles and squares are easiest to cut, but you can get creative with circular windows or arched doors).

4. Cut out windows and doors with the carving knife.

5. Clean off the pumpkin and pat the outside dry (to ensure the hot glue will adhere properly).

6. Hot glue twigs around the windows to frame. Also, poke two twigs into the inner sides of the windows, crossing them vertically and horizontally.

7. Hot glue pinecone scales around the lid of your pumpkin to make the roof. (Start gluing the scales at the base of the lid, then work your way up to the stem in a circular pattern.) As an alternative, you can also use moss or leaves to cover the roof.

8. Decorate your pumpkin home and "yard" with anything you can imagine—figurines, flower planters, ladders, slides, swings, clotheslines, bridges, or stepping-stones.

9. Place a candle (or LED light) in your pumpkin and enjoy the autumnal beauty!

BY ELLE CELAYA

MOTHER
EARTH
WOOL
FELTING

They say that home is where the heart is, and never were words more true. Providing a loving home for our children has nothing to do with the color of our walls or the style of our furniture but is about the memories and moments we create within.

When my husband, Francesco, and I first bought our house, we quickly singled out a space where we wanted to create a large open-plan kitchen that would be the heart of our home. Only, the roof was full of gaping holes, many of the beams had been blackened by fire, and parts of the walls were about to collapse.

And so we got to work—building our dream, one stone at a time. While Francesco enjoyed doing all the dirty work, I was hunting for decorating ideas in magazines filled with glamorous interior designs. My Pinterest feed was dominated by beautiful cottages with whitewashed walls and reclaimed wooden furniture.

But once we started living in our new home, I quickly realized that I didn't want our house to feel like one of the glossy pictures I had admired so much while we were building it. What I wanted instead was for it to feel like home. To us, but also to our children. I wanted them to know that this would be the place they could always come home to, no matter where life would take them. I wanted it to be their haven, just as much as it was ours.

So we made some changes and allowed for life to determine what our house looked like, rather than the other way around. We brought in some cozy carpets for the children to play on, a daybed for living room naps, and I started decorating the house in celebration of the passing seasons, just as I had seen my mother do when I was a child.

We also set up a special corner by the window where we would gather the treasures we brought home from our nature walks. It became a place dedicated to the celebration of nature's beauty, to which each of us could contribute in his or her own special way. It really came to life when I started making little wool-felt scenes, depicting images from our favorite seasonal stories.

Nothing speaks more to the minds and the hearts of our little ones than the stories that we tell.

We're in the thick of autumn—the fallen leaves are whirling in the storm wind, and everything in nature is preparing to go to sleep for winter. For our nature table, I made a special figurine, inspired by Mother Earth when she calls her children home in Sibylle von Olfers's famous book *The Story of the Root Children*. The Mother Earth depicted in this story is a generous caregiver with a loving heart who welcomes her little ones with open arms.

Here, I share a tutorial for how to make your very own Mother Earth.

MATERIALS

Wool batting for the skin color of your choice, as well as 3 earthy colors for the dress and cloak

A small quantity of wool roving to make the hair

Felting needles

A felting mat (or a piece of mattress foam)

Optional: dish soap and water

1 toothpick

1 pipe cleaner

Red wax crayon for the cheeks

 SAFETY TIP

Please be careful when using felting needles, as they're very sharp. Also, always make sure not to change the angle of your needle while it is inserted in your work, or the needle will break.

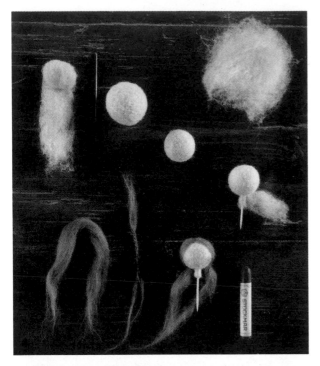

INSTRUCTIONS

MAKING THE HEAD

1. Start by rolling a small amount of your skin-colored wool batting into a tight ball. Don't worry if it doesn't immediately become round; you can adjust that as we go along. Place on the felting mat.

2. Using your thickest felting needle, gently poke around the wool ball to fix the fibers into place. Keep rolling the ball in all directions while you work with the felting needle, so it stays round and won't become flattened on one side. (See page 65, step 4, for more on the felting process.)

3. When all the fibers start looking smooth, take a small quantity of wool batting and tightly wrap it onto the ball, making sure to wrap it in the opposite direction of the wool you have rolled previously. Stab the little ball with your felting needle until it looks smooth.

4. Continue to layer (and felt) thin pieces of wool batting onto the ball until the size looks slightly bigger than you want for your final product. (It will shrink a bit more while you finish felting it.)

5. To create a smooth finish, you can either switch to a finer needle and continue to felt the head until the size is perfect and the surface looks nice and even, or you can proceed by slightly "wet felting" the head.

6. If wet felting, add a tiny amount of soap (a drop of dish soap will do the trick) to a bowl of hot water and dip the ball in. Now gently roll the ball in your hands without squeezing. When you feel the ball is cooling off, dip in hot water again. As you proceed, you will notice that the ball starts to harden. This is when you can start applying a bit more pressure. Gradually, the ball will shrink and become smoother. You can simply stop rolling when it has shrunk to the desired size.

7. Insert the toothpick into the ball.

8. Take a small amount of batting and roll it tightly around the toothpick to create a neck. You can very carefully stab around the neck with your felting needle to secure the fibers and give them a smooth finish if you need to. Also poke upward on the rim between the neck and the head to connect the two parts. Just make sure to work carefully because you could easily break the needle if you hit the toothpick.

9. Next, we're going to create the hair. Take a small amount of roving and fold it in half. Now lay that carefully across the head.

Holding the toothpick in your other hand, arrange the fibers in such a way that they cover the back of the head but not the part of the wool ball that will become the face. (I then take the wool in my left hand, together with the toothpick, so it doesn't move around while I work.)

10. Using your biggest needle, gently felt the roving onto the head. The easiest way to do this is by creating a "midline" in the hair by carefully poking through the roving into the head in a straight line that runs all the way from the face to the nape of the neck. Keep your stabs close together so they create a full line, and all the fibers are held in place.

11. Next, use the tip of your needle to drape the hair as you would like the strands to appear over the back of the head and fasten them with a few easy stabs of your needle at the base of the neck. If you would like, you can create a little braid to wrap around the head. Simply secure it at the nape with a few easy pokes of your felting needle.

12. When the hair is finished, give Mother Earth a healthy glow by painting on some rosy cheeks with a red beeswax crayon.

ROLLING THE ARMS

1. Cut a pipe cleaner to a length of approximately 8 inches.

2. Bend back the tips of the pipe cleaner, so the ends are no longer sharp and won't poke through the wool quite as easily.

3. Take a small piece of skin-colored wool batting, pull it gently to create a wool "ribbon," and wrap that very tightly around one of the tips of the pipe cleaner. If the size and shape look good for a doll's hand, you can secure the fibers by rolling the pipe cleaner with the wool wrapped around it between your hands. If, however, you feel it looks a bit too loose, you can felt the fibers a bit tighter with your needle.

4. Take a small amount of the wool batting in the color you want to use for the upper part of the dress and wrap that tightly around the pipe cleaner (in the same way as you have done to make the hand) to create the arm.

5. Stop at the middle of the pipe cleaner and repeat the last two steps for the other side.

6. When both arms and hands are wrapped, gently bend the pipe cleaner into a horseshoe shape and set it aside until the body is ready for assembling.

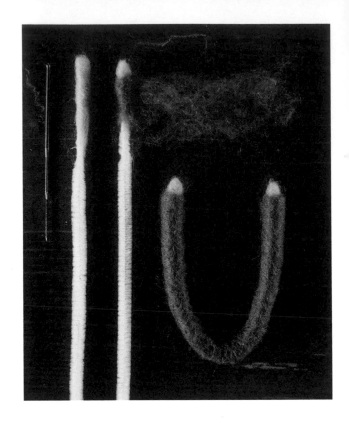

CREATING THE BODY

1. Prepare a thick piece of wool batting in the color you choose for the main part of the dress, approximately 19 inches wide and 8 inches high, and lay it flat onto your working surface.

2. Roll the batting into a cone shape and gently pull away any excess wool. You can also add thin layers of wool if you think some areas need more volume.

3. Use your biggest felting needle to shape the body, emphasizing any areas you want to enhance (such as the top of the body, which will become the bust)—and felting only slightly, just enough to secure the fibers, where the body stays larger, such as the bottom part of the dress.

4. Gently pull out some of the loose fibers of the hem of the dress and fold them over to the bottom. Felt around in circles along the underside to create a flat surface for the doll to stand on.

ASSEMBLING THE DOLL

1. Put the doll in an upright position and insert the end of the toothpick attached to the head into the top of the bust.

2. Lift the head a little bit (so the neck and the bust no longer touch) and place the arms in the space between the body and the head.

3. Now, prepare two small pieces of the wool batting that you had previously chosen for the arms, tug on them gently so they become little wool ribbons, and drape them over the arms to create shoulders and connect the different parts of the body. Make the ribbons overlap crosswise on the front and the back of the body for extra support.

4. Start by needle felting around the neckline and the shoulders, making sure to create connections between all the pieces, until everything stays firmly in place. At this point, you can fray the ends of the wool ribbons to create a blended gradient effect on the dress and finish felting the top of the body with a finer needle.

5. Last, choose a large piece of the third color of batting and drape it around the doll to create a cloak. You can gently felt it in

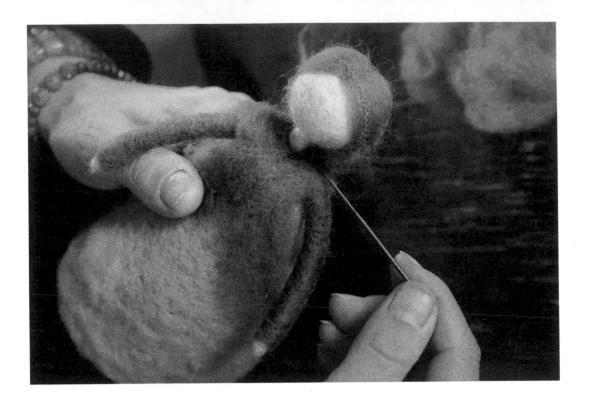

place by stabbing through the batting and into the doll body (for example, on the shoulders) to hold it in place.

And there she is! Your Mother Earth doll is now ready to take up her place in your home. Perhaps you and the children can create a little autumn scene around her with colored leaves, acorns, chestnuts, and other nature treasures. You could even add a few tiny root babies—the seeds of the summer fruits that now return to the land to sleep in their mother's warm embrace.

THE ROOT BABIES: Now that you have mastered all the techniques that we have used to create your Mother Earth doll, you can easily make a few root babies as well. Just start out by making tiny skin-colored felt balls. Next, tightly roll a small amount of wool to create a small log-shaped body. Place the head on top of the body and add a piece of wool over the top of the head to connect the head and the body. Felt everything together, and shape as desired.

BY KATRIEN VAN DEUREN

THE THANKFUL TREE

This season provides an opportunity to reflect on how much we are truly given. I've found that it's so important to cultivate an attitude of thankfulness in our children and nurture this attitude in our own hearts, lest we start taking for granted all that we have. With this in mind, we invited close friends over to our home and held a "thankfulness celebration."

We read *Boxes for Katje* by Candace Fleming, the story of a Dutch girl after World War II whose life is changed by a box of treats and supplies she receives from an American girl, and talked about the simple things that many children in this world go without.

Then we created these lovely "thankful trees," which you can keep adding to for as long as you'd like. They provide a visual reminder of all we have and how we are to share with others.

MATERIALS

One artificial light-up branch (available in most craft stores) and batteries

Clippings from real trees

A quart-size mason jar

Rocks

A leaf punch (mine was 1½ inches) or real leaves to trace

Hole punch

Fall-colored scrapbook paper

String or twine

Fine-tipped marker

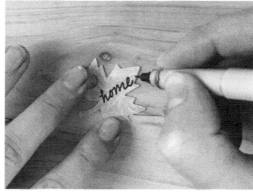

INSTRUCTIONS

1. Place the light-up branch in the mason jar and spread apart to make it look realistic. Add additional real branches and mix them in.

2. Place rocks on the bottom of the jar to hold the branches in place.

3. Use the leaf punch to cut out (or trace if you are using real leaves) as many leaves as you would like out of scrapbook paper. Use the hole punch to add a hole to run the twine through.

4. With the marker, write things you and your family are thankful for on the leaves (for example, we wrote "home," "good books," and "hot cocoa" on a few of ours).

5. Tie a loose knot with twine on each leaf and hang them from the branches.

6. Light up the tree and add daily to your collection of blessings.

BY LEA WU

MOTHERS AS MEMORY MAKERS

BY RACHEL KOVAC

Memories of my childhood Christmases at my Scandinavian grandparents' house are captured in my mind like vivid snapshots. Cinnamon gingerbread boys and girls hung on red satin ribbons from the gray brick mantel of the fireplace, a fire crackling beneath them.

Sometimes I would sit a little too close and a hot ember, glowing red, would land right next to me. I watched my aunts gather to cook and decorate and hang stockings with care. They were shaping my memories and traditions for a lifetime.

As mothers, we are memory makers. This is a high calling, not only to be the shapers of traditions, but also of our children's most dear and cherished memories. When we take that extra step of drawing our children into our traditions, not as observers but as active participants, their memories will be all the more rich and textured, layered with full sensory experiences.

One of the best ways to make our children active participants in our traditions and memories is to make things together. Our children long to make things that are truly useful and beautiful. They delight in seeing the creations of their hands make their way to our windows, our garlands, and our Christmas trees.

As we create together, I hope my children will remember that our Advent season smelled like cinnamon and oranges. It sounded like Handel's Messiah and Christmas jazz. It felt like cinnamon dough in their hands and sticky orange juice on their fingers. It looked like togetherness.

FINDING THE PERFECT TREE

BY CHELSEA HOLLAND

I grew up in rural Alaska with just my parents and big brother, no extended family to speak of for at least three thousand miles. For some, that could seem lonely. Yet my parents took it as a great and wild dare. We would celebrate each and every holiday with gusto. Christmas was no exception, as they went to great lengths to cultivate a holiday filled with traditions and merriment.

I remember my dad tirelessly pulling my brother and me, bundled up in brightly colored puffed snowsuits, in the sled every evening under bright stars. Holiday stories read to us each night before we were tucked in. Homemade hot and flaky crescent rolls slathered in zesty lemon curd sitting atop the table on Christmas morning. By the time I grew up and had a family of my own, I was ready to create our own magical Christmas traditions.

I took on this task with a lot of ambitious ideas. First among them was searching for the perfect tree. Visions swirled in my head of holiday music softly playing, hot cider at the ready, and children bundled in cozy blankets while we ambled over the farm seeking our family room's crowning jewel.

It did not take long, however, for reality to set in.

Picture children piled on top of one another yelling wildly. An endless hike, eyes scanning the distance for "the one," which, when finally found, will inevitably and in true Griswold

fashion be at least double the height of our ceiling. After a tedious wrestling match between human and bush, we load it into the back of the ol' pickup, only to have it bounce out of the bed and career down the hillside on the drive back home. True story.

Yet, we press on.

Sometimes in practice, traditions fall far short of the ideal we dreamed and imagined, but they are fundamental to our sense of who we are. Traditions bring comfort. They add a sense of belonging, reminding us that we are a part of something bigger.

There is something awe-inspiring about how practicing traditions, even imperfectly, creates lasting memories, so that when our kids are all grown up and have sweet children of their own, they have the same desire to put their families first.

My dad may have cursed the snow while he pulled us in the sled. My parents possibly argued over who would read the holiday story and who would wash the dishes. Perhaps my mom burned her first attempt at the crescent rolls. But if so, I don't remember those parts. Our traditions, flawed as they might be, become greater than the sum of their imperfect parts.

And if the missteps are indeed what my children will remember, oh the stories they will have. "Remember that time our Christmas tree fell out of the truck and down the hill?"

What are the most memorable holiday traditions from your childhood? Do you remember any of the things that went wrong? What do you want your children to remember about your holidays together?

A PICTURE BOOK CHRISTMAS

Traditions fill us with nostalgia and joy during the holidays. Setting up a tree, listening to Christmas music, waking up to filled stockings, eating cinnamon rolls. In many ways, the traditions make the holiday.

That's why I always loved the idea of reading one Christmas book a day leading up to December 25. The thought of wrapping twenty-five books every year, however, was overwhelming.

Last year I came across this lovely idea to decorate muslin bags as reusable "wrappings" for the Christmas books, and I knew this finishing touch would complete my vision for this tradition. So we purchased twenty-five muslin bags and made an afternoon out of stamping the bags while listening to *The Nutcracker*.

I painted numerals on each of the bags and filled them with books. (Some days have more than one.) And now, we excitedly await each new day in December to open a bag and see what goodies await us.

MATERIALS

25 muslin bags (I used 12 × 16-inch bags)

Christmas or winter stamps

Black ink pad

Paint

Paintbrush

**25 (or more!) Christmas books
(see page 30 for book ideas)**

INSTRUCTIONS

1. With the stamps and ink pad, stamp as much as you like on each muslin bag.

2. With the paintbrush, paint a numeral from 1 to 25 on each bag.

3. Fill each bag with one (or two!) books.

4. On each day in December leading up to Christmas, open up the day's bag, and read the book with your children!

BY ALISHA MILLER

OUR FAVORITE CHRISTMAS BOOKS

Apple Tree Christmas
by Trinka Hakes Noble

The Fir Tree
by Hans Christian Andersen

The Little Shepherd Girl
by Juliann Henry

Voices of Christmas
by Nikki Grimes

The Legend of St. Nicholas
by Dandi Daley Mackall

The Tomten
by Astrid Lindgren

Christmas Trolls
by Jan Brett

A Certain Small Shepherd
by Rebecca Caudill

Big Susan
by Elizabeth Orton Jones

The Year of the Perfect
Christmas Tree
by Gloria Houston

The Crippled Lamb
by Max Lucado

The Third Gift
by Linda Sue Park

Annika's Secret Wish
by Beverly Lewis

The Christmas Miracle of
Jonathan Toomey
by Susan Wojciechowski

Lucia Morning in Sweden
by Ewa Rydaker

Carl's Christmas
by Alexandra Day

Christmas Farm
by Mary Lyn Ray

The Legend of the
Poinsettia
by Tomie dePaola

Song of the Stars
by Sally Lloyd-Jones

The Story of Holly & Ivy
by Rumer Godden

The Little Drummer Boy
by Ezra Jack Keats

The Story of Christmas
by Pamela Dalton (Illustrator)

Christmas Day in
the Morning
by Pearl S. Buck

Mr. Willowby's
Christmas Tree
by Robert Barry

Silent Night:
The Song and Its Story
by Margaret Hodges

The Night Before Christmas
by Clement C. Moore
(illustrated by Gyo Fujikawa)

The Twelve Days of
Christmas
by Laurel Long

The Gift of the Magi
by O. Henry (illustrated by
Lisbeth Zwerger)

We Three Kings
by Gennady Spirin

The Candymaker's Gift
by Helen and David Haidle

The Remarkable Christmas
of the Cobbler's Sons
by Ruth Sawyer

Room for a Little One
by Martin Waddell

Bright Christmas:
An Angel Remembers
by Andrew Clements

The Nutcracker
by E. T. A. Hoffman
(illustrated by
Lisbeth Zwerger)

A CELEBRATION OF LIGHT

As a child, I was fascinated by my family's cultural heritage. I wanted to know more about my ancestors who came by boat from England in the 1700s, about my babi's parents who emigrated from Czechoslovakia, and about my great-grandmother Anna Nordgren, whose family came from Sweden to Canada and then the United States.

It was this desire to know my place in the world that led me to research the customs of my Scandinavian relatives and, in turn, ignited my love for Sankta Lucia.

Sankta Lucia, or Saint Lucy, as she is known in the English-speaking world, is a central and beloved figure in Swedish cultural lore. On December 13, her feast day, sweet treats are baked, children don costumes and visit neighbors, and communities attend Lucia processions in schools, businesses, and churches.

Born in the third century CE in Southern Italy, Lucia would have disappeared into the annals of history but for her courage to speak up for her faith and her insistence on doing good for the poor. These convictions led Lucia to refuse a marriage proposal, devote her life to service, and ultimately become a martyr for her faith.

Many years later, Lucia was canonized as a saint for her courageous acts of love and care.

But how did an Italian-born saint become the focus of a Scandinavian celebration? Well, that is a bit of a mystery. The story most commonly told is that during a terrible famine in the Middle Ages, on December 13, something miraculous transpired.

A beautiful young woman dressed in white and wearing a wreath of candles on her head traveled by lighted boat to bring the people of Sweden lifesaving grain. The Swedish citizens believed the woman to be Sankta Lucia herself. From this miraculous light-filled beginning came one of the most beautiful and festive celebrations in Scandinavia.

Now, every December 13, children dress in long white gowns and serve their families and neighbors pepparkakor (gingersnaps) and coffee. The eldest girl plays the role of Lucia and wears a red sash and a crown of candles. The younger girls serve as Lucia's attendants and carry single candles. Boys play the part of Star Boy, wearing pointed hats and carrying star wands, to spread light on the celebration.

Sometimes toddlers dress as gingerbread cookies, adding a sweet and silly element to the festivities. In Sweden and in parts of the world with large Scandinavian populations, public Lucia processions are held. These celebrations include caroling, scripture reading, food, and fellowship.

The themes of light and service in Lucia's narrative are a perfect foil to the long, dark, and cold nights of winter. Bringing light to those in need can be a springboard for our own families' celebration of Lucia Day. Creating a Lucia Fest in our homes can be as simple as taking cookies to an elderly neighbor or as elaborate as dressing in traditional costumes, telling Lucia's story, and creating a processional complete with carols and candles.

In whatever celebration you choose, may the story of Lucia, her insistence on doing good, and her devotion to her faith dispel the darkness and fill your heart and home with light.

IDEAS FOR LUCIA FEST

HERE ARE A FEW IDEAS FOR CREATING YOUR OWN LUCIA FEST AT HOME:

1. Learn more about Lucia and her story through high-quality books, such as *Lucia Morning in Sweden* by Ewa Rydaker, and *Lucia, Child of Light* by Florence Ekstrand.

2. Purchase or sew white gowns—Lucia gowns for girls and Star Boy gowns for boys. Create wreaths and conical hats or purchase a premade Lucia crown and Star Boy hat and wand kit.

3. Bake pepparkakor (gingersnaps)—see following page for a recipe. Alternately, you can purchase them from IKEA or your local Scandinavian store's grocery section.

4. Learn a few simple Lucia carols. "Lusse Lelle" and "Godor Afton" are easy and fun! You can easily find Swedish and English lyrics for the traditional Neapolitan tune "Sankta Lucia" (*Natten går tunga fjät*).

5. Visit an elderly neighbor or friend. Share your sweet treats, songs, and the story of Lucia. Ask them about their childhood holiday traditions.

6. Contact local Scandinavian or Nordic organizations and inquire about community-wide Lucia Fests.

7. Use Lucia Day as a time to catch your breath during a busy holiday season. Focus on the themes of light and service as you prepare for the long winter ahead.

PEPPARKAKOR

(GINGERSNAPS)

This recipe comes from The Wooden Spoon in Plano, Texas.

INGREDIENTS

1½ cups Crisco

2 cups white sugar
(plus additional for rolling)

2 eggs

¼ cup molasses

½ teaspoon salt

2 teaspoons cinnamon

1 teaspoon cloves

¾ teaspoon ginger

2 teaspoons baking soda

4 cups flour

1. Cream together the Crisco and the sugar until combined.

2. Add the eggs and molasses, mixing well after each addition.

3. Add the salt, spices, and baking soda, then the flour, one cup at a time. Mix until there are no streaks of flour. Dough with be stiff.

4. Take a tablespoon of dough, roll into a ball, roll the ball in white sugar, and place spaced a couple inches apart on an ungreased cookie sheet. Repeat with all of the dough.

5. Bake at 350°F for 10 to 12 minutes.

BY AMANDA GREGG

WINTER
TABLE PIECE

In our family, we celebrate the yearly festivals that mark the passing of the seasons. It is our way to celebrate the gift of being together and to connect with the rhythm of all that surrounds us. We mark the coming of spring after a long dark winter and the wild abundance of summer, the quieting of nature around the fall equinox, and then finally winter and the birth of light.

As with many things, an important part of the joy lies in the anticipation, the preparation for the events that are approaching. That's why we work together with our boys to craft seasonally inspired decorations—a tradition that not only adds a festive note to the seasonal mood of our living space but also allows them to actively take part in the festive commemoration of life's ever-flowing cycles. I especially like it when we can craft seasonal decorations with elements that we have brought back from one of our many walks in the woods.

Here I will share some tips on how to craft your very own winter table piece. It's a simple craft you can work on together as a family and that can easily be styled to match the way your family celebrates the midwinter festivities. And why not start with a nature walk? It's the perfect opportunity to reflect on how everything changes around us now that the darker days of the year are upon us and to gather some materials you can use in your winter decoration piece.

MATERIALS

Six or seven small log stubs,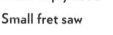
cut to different lengths

Pinecones, moss, rose hips,
pretty crystals, rocks, etc.

Piece of plywood

Small fret saw

Medium grit sanding paper
(e.g., grit P100)

Water-based paint and a paintbrush

Mod Podge–style glue, or wood glue

Paintbrush for the glue

Decorations of your choice

Small candle holder, or a ¾-inch
(or ⅞-inch) spade drill bit

Taper candle of the appropriate size
for your candle holder

Optional: woodworking clamps

SAFETY TIP

Using saws and drills can be dangerous and should be done with adult supervision.

PREPARATIONS: Depending on the ages of your children, you might want to prepare some of the elements in advance. My boys are both five, so we went out into the woods, where they chose a branch and cut it down on their own. My husband, Francesco, later sawed it into little stubs for them.

He also prepared a candle holder, using a 7/8-inch spade drill bit to make a hole in a short stub of wood. Of course, you can always skip this step by using a small candle holder if you have one.

INSTRUCTIONS

1. Using a drafting compass or a large bowl or plate turned upside down as a template, draw a circle of approximately 11 inches onto your piece of plywood.

2. Fasten the plywood onto your table or workbench using woodworking clamps, and use the fret saw to cut out the circle. Don't worry if you don't have any woodworking clamps. You can simply help your child by firmly holding the plywood down onto the working surface while they use the saw.

3. If the edges of your circle are jagged, smooth them with sanding paper.

4. If you don't like the color of the plywood, you can easily color it with some of your regular water-based paint. (I wanted our table piece to match the wood of our dinner table, so we painted it dark brown and dried it with a hair dryer in order to get right back to work.)

5. Arrange the different stubs along one side of the plywood circle and glue them into place using the wood glue and brush.

6. Place the small candle holder in front of the stubs, insert a candle into the holder, and cover the rest of the circle with the moss. Apply glue as needed.

7. Decorate your winter piece with some of your nature treasures and then add a few other small decorations as well, such as some wooden animals and felt figurines to recount your favorite winter tale. Or why not add a few of your heirloom Christmas ornaments? You can even keep the piece through the whole winter and gradually change the decorations to match the passing of the season. The possibilities are limitless.

8. Remember to never leave the candle burning unattended.

BY KATRIEN VAN DEUREN

NATURAL
CHRISTMAS
TREE

A few years ago, my children asked if they could decorate our Christmas tree entirely with natural ornaments, and they loved it so much that it has become an annual tradition. Other than slicing oranges, my children make the ornaments entirely by themselves. They are the visionaries and the creators.

The ornaments are natural and simple, yet beautiful. The ingredients are inexpensive and when the Christmas season is over, all the ornaments can be composted, making them gentle on our planet too. I love that I don't have to worry about glass or precious ornaments being shattered by little hands. Even our toddler joins in the fun of hanging (and moving and hanging again!) these ornaments.

Here are our family's favorite recipes. You can also find instruction for making a popcorn garland on page 67, which would be a lovely addition to these trees.

SAFETY TIP

Using the oven and sharp knives can be dangerous and should be done with adult supervision.

INSTRUCTIONS

1. Preheat oven to 200°F.

2. Mix the cinnamon and applesauce together in a bowl until the dough forms a soft, smooth ball. If the dough feels too dry, add a bit more applesauce. If it feels too sticky, add a little more cinnamon.

3. Section the dough into four equal parts. Roll one section out on a piece of parchment paper until it's ¼-inch thick.

4. Use cookie cutters to cut out your ornaments.

5. Place the ornaments on a smooth baking sheet lined with parchment paper.

6. Make a hole at the top of each ornament with a toothpick, pencil, or chopstick. (Don't forget this step! You need the hole to be able to hang your ornaments!)

7. Repeat with the other three sections of dough.

8. Bake for 2½ hours until firm.

9. Let cool on a wire rack overnight.

10. Hang with a pretty piece of ribbon, baker's twine, or jute twine.

CINNAMON ORNAMENTS

MATERIALS

2½ cups cinnamon

1½ cups applesauce

Cookie cutters (can be any shape you like, but holiday-themed ones are festive)

Toothpick, pencil, or chopstick

Jute twine, thin ribbon, or baker's twine

WHOLE DRIED ORANGES

MATERIALS

Whole oranges or tangerines

A sharp knife

Jute twine, baker's twine, or ribbon

A bobby pin or needle

INSTRUCTIONS

1. Preheat your oven to 180°F.

2. Place your orange on a chopping board so the stem is on top. Think of the stem as the north pole and the bottom of the orange like the south pole.

3. Using a sharp knife, slice the orange through the peel only. Start at the north pole and slice down to the south pole, leaving a bit of the peel intact at both the top and bottom of the orange. Make four equidistant cuts this way, slicing through the peel only. Your orange will now be quartered into four equal sections while remaining intact at the top and bottom.

4. Next, slice, also from north to south, in between each of the four quarters, creating eight equal-size segments, continuing to preserve the peel at the top and bottom of your poles. Make sure you slice all the way through the peel. This is very important in the baking and drying process.

5. Place the oranges on a baking sheet lined with parchment paper. Then place in the oven to bake and dry for 12 to 24 hours. Rotate the oranges every few hours. You will know when your oranges are done when they feel significantly lighter and begin to brown but not burn.

6. Let cool on a wire rack overnight.

7. Once completely cool, create a hanging loop using your favorite twine or ribbon. You can thread the twine or ribbon through the closed end of a bobby pin or a needle to help you poke it through the orange.

ORANGE SLICES

MATERIALS

Oranges

A sharp knife

Jute twine, baker's twine, or ribbon

A bobby pin

INSTRUCTIONS

1. Choose oranges with vibrant colors! (You could also use lemons or grapefruit for added variety in size and color.)

2. Preheat the oven to 250°F.

3. Using a sharp knife, slice the oranges crosswise in ⅛-inch to ¼-inch rounds, taking care to slice them evenly.

4. Place them on a paper towel. Then carefully pat them dry on both sides using a paper towel or cloth. This step is very important! My children love to pat the orange slices dry while I do the slicing.

5. Place the orange slices on a smooth baking sheet lined with parchment paper.

6. Bake for 2½ hours, flipping every 30 minutes.

7. Remove the orange slices when they begin to brown slightly.

8. Cool on a wire rack.

9. After the slices are fully cooled, create a hanging loop with twine or ribbon. We like to thread the twine through the closed end of a bobby pin and create a hole in the orange slice using the bobby pin.

BY RACHEL KOVAC

TURNING ARTWORK INTO FESTIVE DECOR

Our family does a lot of drawing, particularly in our nature journals, where we draw plants, creatures, and landscapes we've observed. Drawing is a skill to be built upon, so we love to look back often to see how we've grown and progressed as artists.

Remembering and reflecting on our past drawings is a wonderful practice for each of us. To highlight and celebrate the growth we've seen, this Christmas season, my family created festive ornaments from my children's artwork.

The process is fairly simple and something you can do with your own children (some adult participation and supervision is needed). Their faces will light up when they see their artwork on display, and you will have forever keepsakes of these sweet years together.

MATERIALS

Mod Podge

1-inch-wide paintbrush

**Slices of wood
(from a craft store or homemade)**

Twine or ribbon

Scissors

Artwork

 SAFETY TIP

Scissors can be dangerous and should be used with adult supervision.

INSTRUCTIONS

1. Find some of your children's artwork or doodles and take a photo. If they're too young to have done drawings of their own, find something they've colored in a coloring book.

2. Use any photo-editing software you choose to clean up the images a bit. I use an app on my phone called Snapseed. Others that could work include Capture One, PicMonkey, GIMP, Canva, Adobe Photoshop, or Adobe Lightroom.

3. Print the works of art in various sizes. (I knew I wanted to adhere their artwork to small pieces of wood, so I printed a few different sheets accordingly.)

4. Once printed, use scissors to cut around the artwork. The kiddos can jump in and help. We left a white border to help the images stand out from the wood background. No need for perfection here. Our children's little snips add so much character to the finished piece.

5. Use the woodcuts as backgrounds for the artwork. These wooden pieces are just cross-sections of small logs, sectioned in about ¼-inch-thick segments with a tiny hole drilled through in order to slip a piece of twine or decorative ribbon for hanging. If you're not up to making your own, the big

craft stores have selections. Use ribbon or twine for hanging.

6. With your Mod Podge and a 1-inch-wide paintbrush, paint the surface of one side of the wood. Then carefully place the drawing on the wet surface and smooth out any wrinkles. Paint another layer of Mod Podge over the top. Set aside to dry. (A word of caution: depending on the age of your kids, you'll have to determine how much they can help with this step. Mod Podge is quite sticky and not very forgiving if the paper artwork needs to be moved.)

7. After your piece is dry, repeat this process on the opposite side to add more artwork.

8. Allow the finished products an hour or two to dry, and then you'll have some precious festive mementos to display for years to come. Hang them on a tree. Use them as garlands across your fireplace or a window, or even down a stairwell.

BY HEIDI EITREIM

COLLECTING ORNAMENTS

BY KIRSTY LARMOUR

Our family travels a lot, and one of our favorite traditions is collecting a Christmas ornament from each place we visit. From felted Christmas trees made by yurt-living nomads in Kyrgyzstan and painted ceramics from Poland to candy canes from the USA and camels from the Middle East, each of these ornaments comes with a set of memories.

As we decorate our tree each year, it's a time to pause and reflect and relive some of the experiences that bind us together as a family. The kids remember "the best hot chocolate ever at the Christmas market in Romania" or how "it rained so much that day and we had to huddle under one umbrella."

Some of the ornaments also give us a chance to think about loved ones far away, as we know each of them has an Abu Dhabi camel ornament that we gave them hanging on their tree. We often spend all day dressing the tree as we relive stories from over the years, and I love the way this annual practice becomes woven into our family traditions.

What ornaments do you remember best from your childhood Christmas tree? What ornaments do your children get the most excited about hanging from the tree? Which ones spark a story or reminiscence?

HAND-EMBROIDERED STAR

B ecause home is our haven, our safety net, and our place of refuge when the world is too much to handle, it should be filled with items that bring us peace, evoke joy, or tell a story.

When the weather gets colder, my family turns toward handcrafts. After taking in as much as we can of the gray skies and the cold air biting our cheeks, we rest in the warmth from our fireplace, the bright fire reflecting in our eyes as we focus on the gentle and steady work of our hands.

For me, this is a precious time to hold littles on my lap, breathe in their scents, whisper quietly in their ears, and guide their little hands. We make these mementos because it draws us nearer together, and afterward my children can proudly gift their finished art or display it lovingly in our home.

Please enjoy this delicate hand-embroidered piece that can be used as a Christmas decoration, ornament, place setting, or whatever else you deem worthy in your haven of rest.

MATERIALS

**Embroidery hoop
(mine was 4 inches in diameter)**

Cotton or linen fabric cut to size

Scissors

Embroidery floss and needle

Fine-tipped Sharpie marker

SAFETY TIP

Embroidery needles and scissors can be dangerous and should be used with adult supervision.

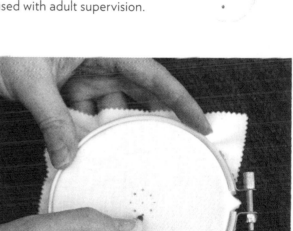

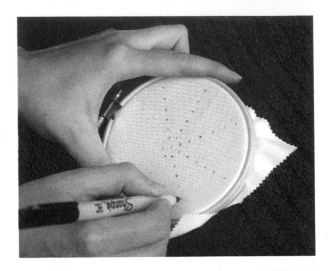

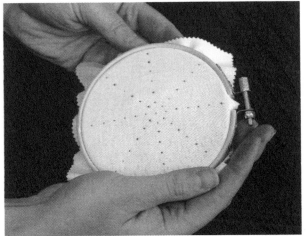

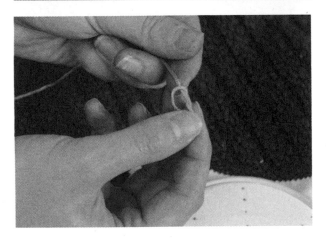

INSTRUCTIONS

1. Tighten fabric inside the embroidery hoop.

2. Draw, very faintly, one small dot in the center of the fabric with the Sharpie. (Make sure it's faint because you will see this dot at the end of the project.)

3. Draw eight dots around the middle one in a circular shape. Then, for each of the eight outer dots, draw five more dots extending outward from the center dot toward the hoop frame to form a sort of "ray." There should be six dots total in each ray.

4. Use the scissors to cut about two arms' lengths worth of embroidery floss. Tie a small knot at one end, and at the other end thread your needle, but make sure NOT to tie a knot on this end (it is hard to pull through the fabric).

5. Start with your needle coming from the fabric bottom through to the top at the outermost end of any ray of your choice (we'll call it ray 1). Poke a hole going toward the fabric bottom into the first dot from the center on the ray to the left (ray 2).

6. Poke a hole up through ray 1, the dot second to the outermost point, and thread it toward the bottom through the second dot

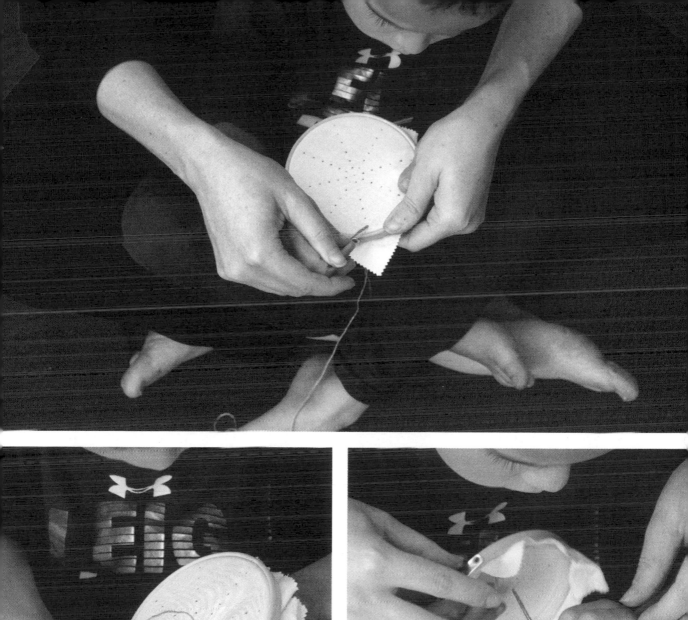

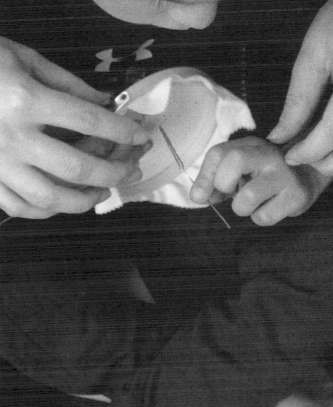

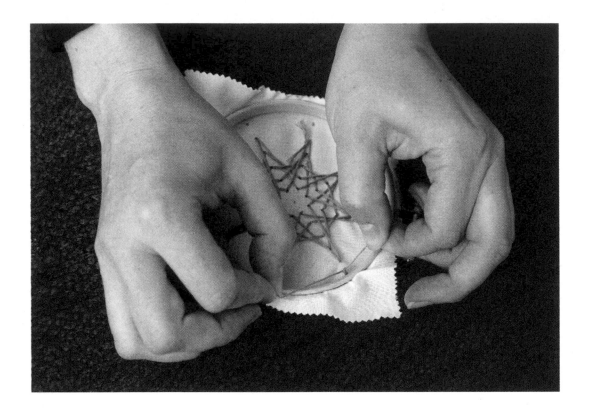

from the middle on ray 2. As we work our way down ray 1, we are threading up ray 2.

7. When you have finished this pattern, it will look like a "V" or a curve using all straight lines.

8. To move into the next "V" to the left, poke a hole coming up slightly above the dot on the end of ray 2 (not exactly in the same spot), and continue the pattern of

going to the first dot toward the center, now going to ray 3.

9. If you need more embroidery floss, find a place on the back to tie a knot. When done, trim off the edges of the fabric if you wish to keep it displayed in the embroidery hoop.

10. This star is a total of eight "Vs" and will look stunning when complete!

BY LEA WU

HOW TO DRAW A CHRISTMAS WREATH

have heard it said that simple things, repeated over and over again, make lasting memories. Isn't that encouraging? No matter our level of expertise or the limits of the materials we have at hand, we can all create worthy memories from this time together with our families.

Here is a simple tutorial for drawing a Christmas wreath. It's something you can do with your children while baking cookies in the oven or playing soothing Christmas music in the living room.

I chose to draw this wreath with a Micron pen instead of a pencil. I knew this wreath would be made of lots of simple lines, and I didn't want to have to retrace everything. The great thing about using Micron pens is that they will not bleed when you paint over them with watercolor.

MATERIALS

Micron pen or pencil
Drawing paper
Watercolor paints
Small paintbrush(es)
Optional: poem

INSTRUCTIONS

1. Use the pen or pencil to trace a bowl on the paper to get a perfectly round circle for your wreath.

2. Draw the leaves for your design. I chose to work with four or five shapes with very simple lines. You can change the shape of the leaves slightly to bring a bit more diversity.

3. Continue the design all the way around the wreath. Go back and add more berries or tiny leaves where it needs more filling.

4. You can fill in the center of the wreath with a poem, song lyrics, or something meaningful to you. I decided to copy a poem from Nancy Willard in the center of my wreath.

5. Using a small paintbrush, fill in your leaves and berries with watercolors. I kept my painting color choices to a minimum, starting with my lightest shades of green and rust colors and layering on from there until I loved the look. Using the leftover rust color in my palette, I added a lot of water and painted a light color around the full wreath to give a frame feel to the page.

BY KRISTIN ROGERS

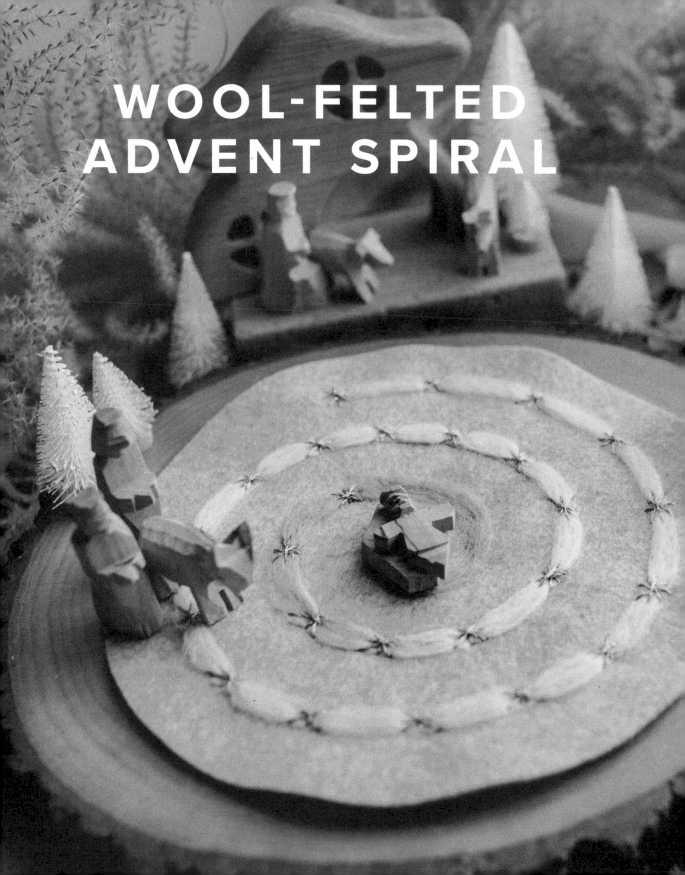

WOOL-FELTED ADVENT SPIRAL

This last wintry month of the year rarely feels like an ending to me but rather a glittering bend in the calming spiral of nature's rhythmic cycles. We nurture ourselves and our children with rich spices and soups, supportive immune tinctures, and soft wool socks against the chill of hardwood floors and icy drafts. Our souls are sustained with stories spun by firelight and the sound of snow falling upon snow.

Even in the midst of this healing, inward pull, we are still easily enticed by the sparkle of holiday flair. Our desire to cast a wide net of gorgeous and meaningful experiences, along with our eagerness to go to great lengths to procure treasures to present to our children, can sometimes culminate in holiday burnout.

I encourage all of us to discern the worthy traditions amid the roar of the holiday noise and say "No thank you" to the activities that don't serve our best interests during this sacred time. I know in my heart

that, especially for young children, it isn't the new and flashy holiday surprises that form the best memories, but rather the familiarity of simple, recurring traditions: the same wonky ornaments unwrapped year after year from the attic, the same maple-syrup candy poured on the first snowfall, and the quiet Yule log at the winter solstice.

Quite a few years ago, my boys and I made a homemade salt-dough spiral as a centerpiece for our simple Advent traditions. The symbol of the spiral has been traditionally associated with rebirth, the passing of seasons and time, or a spiritual journey.

This year, we decided to create an Advent spiral crafted from wool and thread, handmade from simple and natural materials, yet durable and safe enough for all ages. We chose to sew twenty-five stars for our family to count down to Christmas day, adding to this centerpiece small nature treasure decorations on each of the four Advent Sundays before Christmas.

The number of stars on this spiral could also be changed to count down to any alternate celebrations, such as the winter solstice or New Year's Eve.

May you lean into the quiet inner work of this season and gently remind your spirit that even the simplest things you do in mindfulness and love are bringing light to your children's hearts.

MATERIALS

Large piece of wool felt (big enough to cut into a circle about a foot in diameter)

Colored (or natural) wool roving

Felting needle

Felting surface such as a foam block or sponge

Gold thread

Sewing needle

Scissors

Optional: pencil

Felting needles and scissors can be dangerous and should be used with adult supervision.

INSTRUCTIONS

1. Using scissors, cut your piece of wool felt into a circle with about a 12-inch diameter. (You could use a math compass, but we turned a large mixing bowl upside down and traced the outline to get the shape and size we wanted.)

2. Gently separate your bunches of wool roving into long, wispy strands that are all approximately the same width.

3. Lay your strands clockwise around the circle of wool felt, overlapping their ends slightly so that they form a gradual spiral "path" toward the center. (My son started with lighter cream colors on the outside and worked toward darker winter blues on the inside of the spiral.)

4. Lay the entire circle on top of your felting foam or surface and slowly begin the process of "felting" by repeatedly poking your needle straight up and down over the strands of roving. This will condense and press the wool fibers together until they are interlocked and begin to bind with the felt circle beneath.

NOTE: You may need to pause and use the fingers on your opposite hand to guide some of the stray pieces back into the path of the spiral that you are trying to create. But make sure to keep those fingers well out of the way of the needle when you are actively poking so they don't get accidentally speared! This is certainly a process that requires careful supervision for younger children.

5. Once you have finished felting, cut a long length of gold thread and pass it through the eye of your needle, tying a strong knot at the end.

6. Begin embroidering your chosen number of "stars" along the top of the spiral path. (To ensure a general evenness in spacing, it may help to mark the location of each star with a small pencil dot prior to

sewing.) When you are finished sewing, tie off the thread underneath your Advent spiral and cut off any excess.

7. Find a charming place to display your handiwork and enjoy the interactive countdown to the coming of the light!

BY LEAH DAMON

CHRISTMAS
GARLAND

My family made homemade Christmas tree garlands and ornaments a few years ago, and it has grown into an annual tradition. I delight in creating a warm and inviting ambience for all occasions in my home, and our Christmas celebration begins with this special craft day. I light a cranberry- or pine-scented candle, warm a pot of wassail, and stream Christmas carols throughout the house.

These garlands of dried oranges, cranberries, and popcorn were inspired by a children's storybook called *Night Tree* by Eve Bunting. In this story, a family embarks on their annual tradition to decorate a tree in the forest. But instead of using typical decorations, they make garlands and ornaments with food items. The decorations are then left for the animals to feast on.

Wanting to embrace this idea, I found ways to adapt it for my family and have each of my children participate. My bigger kids help me slice oranges and thread the needles, while my toddler loves eating the popcorn and dancing to the Christmas music.

MATERIALS

A sharp knife

Large oranges (6 to 8)

A bag of cranberries

A few bags of plain microwave popcorn

Needle

Sewing thread

Fishing line

 SAFETY TIP

Using an oven, sewing needles, and knife can be dangerous and should be done with adult supervision.

INSTRUCTIONS

1. Preheat the oven to 200°F.

2. Using the knife, start by cutting the oranges into thin, even slices. Dry them in the oven by placing them directly on the oven rack. Thin slices will dry in one to two hours. Thicker slices will take three to four hours. Flip halfway.

3. Dry cranberries by spreading them on a paper towel and leaving them to dry for a few hours.

4. Make popcorn.

5. Thread a needle on either the fishing line or sewing thread, and begin threading the oranges, cranberries, and popcorn in your desired pattern. To thread the oranges, sew in and out across the top of each orange slice so it will lie flat.

6. Knot ends when completed and hang on your tree, mantel, or shelf for a festive holiday decoration.

The versatility of this garland allows you the choice to adorn your mantel, spruce up your Christmas tree, or leave it in the forest for the animals. I know your family will take pride in creating something beautiful together while making memories that will last a lifetime.

BY CAROL ANN SARTELL

TIPS FOR ORNAMENTS

- You may need to experiment with different materials for sewing. Sewing thread may not hold heavier fruit, and fishing line may break the popcorn when attempting to thread it.

- If you do not have oranges, this garland works well and looks great strung across the tree with just popcorn and cranberries.

- For an easy ornament, tie some thread or fishing line through a dried orange slice and add a small piece of cinnamon stick, clove, or greenery tied in with it.

A MOTHER'S SEARCH FOR LIGHT

BY LEAH BODEN

I recently bought a string of outdoor lights to hang across the trees in my backyard. As the nights draw in and our days seem so much shorter, I needed a glimmer of light dotted in the distance to break up the monotony of the night. Now when I engage in my morning rhythm of creeping downstairs to pour a cup of tea before anyone else is awake, I flick on the switch and enjoy the lights. This ritual has done wonders for my soul.

In each changing season, in the midst of seeking to cultivate the souls of our children, we would do well to create a habit that stills our own souls and creates calm.

I'm an avid light chaser all year round, but I've come to realize that as autumn turns to winter, I have a particularly strong need to see it, create it, linger in it, and show it to others.

I light a tealight and place it in a jar that sits on the picnic bench at the front of our home to welcome visitors. I light a candle in the porch as family members leave while it's still dark in the morning so that the last thing they see is light. I point out sunrises and sunsets, stars and sky to my children from inside our home and out. I light lamps next to bookshelves and throw fairy lights over picture frames because now is a better time than ever to illuminate life.

The search for light settles into our winter rhythms and divides our day as we routinely strike a match to illuminate a window, blow on embers as friends gather around a chiminea with stories and hot chocolate, and reach for headlamps and flashlights to once more go out into the night.

When the morning light is bright, we sit by the bay window overlooking the park with a stack of books and a pot of tea—time for lingering and doodling while listening to festive tales by Dickens and Tolkien, Brothers Grimm and Hans Christian Andersen.

From my desk where I write, I see a shaft of bright blue sky break through the gray of the day and the remaining red, orange, and yellow leaves fall to the ground, bidding autumn a final farewell.

The sunset's glistening routine catches my eye in the breakfast room at the end of the day, and I snap a picture of its illuminating dance across the wooden shelves holding plants and jugs and memories. It only lasts a moment but deserves my attention.

The oven is warm and glowing in the darkening kitchen, exuding aromas of breads and cookies and pies as older children walk in from their cold day away from home, declaring, "That smells amazing! What is it? I'm starving."

We light fires and candles and spaces. The summer bunting turns to festive banners, and baubles are hung with care to sparkle and spin on a tree because maybe all of us in this yuletide season are fueling our souls, adjusting our sight, and looking, really looking, for light.

SNOWFLAKE ART

We stopped for breakfast at the quaint little diner. We had coffee and these amazing pancake dippers, deepfried.

"... but now the snow had added an extra layer of silence, as though the entire area had been soundproofed." pg 25

A Year in Provence

*Today the word buffalo is a widely accepted term for American bison."

Bison

They are both members of the cattle family but buffalo are different and live on another continent. Africa, South Asia.

Bryce canyon

Tunnel

Thunderbird Cafe

Blondies Diner

We live in California and don't typically have a true "winter" like other states, which is why we decided to take a winter trip to Zion National Park in southwest Utah.

We traveled to Utah to see snow, but soon after we arrived at the home we had rented, so much snow fell that the roads closed, and we weren't able to drive into the park and were stuck on the property.

At first, we did our best to be purposeful with our girls' indoor time. I read them books, provided paper for them to draw on, and we wrote in our nature journals. We played music and let them mess up their room and drink hot chocolate. And we looked through our field guide to try to identify animals or tracks we could see from the windows.

Yet there was only so much we could do indoors, and we eventually suited up in boots, snow pants, coats, scarves, and hats and set out to explore the snowy world outside our door. Each night around evening time, we watched the ducks waddle over to the pond, quack loudly, and splash in the frigid water, to the delight of my youngest daughter. She was also amazed by the massive, majestic bison we were able to see up close, with just a wooden fence between us.

My eldest daughter spotted bunny tracks in the snow and followed them until she found a white bunny eating under a tree. To my shock, it let her walk over and pick it up. She cuddled it and set it down, and it kept right on eating.

Their favorite memories from the trip were these outside experiences, walking over to see the animals on the property and climbing huge snow piles.

It would have been much easier to keep them inside, dry and warm, but it was worth every effort to get them outside to experience all those life-giving, simple moments in nature. These precious outdoor moments offer endless inspiration for indoor reflection and nature journaling.

For those moments when winter storms make it impossible to get out in nature, here's a tutorial for drawing snowflakes:

MATERIALS

Drawing paper
Pencil
Watercolor paints
Small paintbrushes
Optional: Micron pen

INSTRUCTIONS

1. Make the outline of the snowflake with pencil on your paper. Don't worry about making your lines perfectly symmetrical.

2. Mix a color you desire for your snowflake, starting with the lightest shade first. I wanted my paint to look very watery and imperfect, so I left quite a bit of water on my brush. Let the water spread how it wants to get those loose edges.

3. Let your snowflake dry. This will take a bit longer due to the additional amount of water you're using.

4. Mix a slightly darker color for the center and the dots on the edge of the snowflake.

5. Let it dry.

NOTE: Typically, I would use a Micron pen to add the final touches, but I left it out this time to create a more liquid, less defined feel.

BY KRISTIN ROGERS

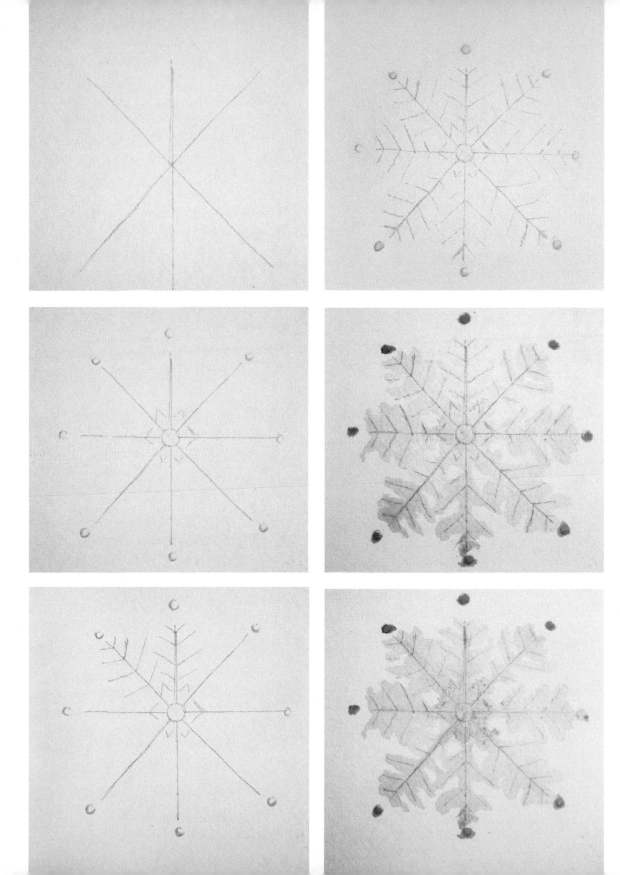

ARROZ CON LECHE

BY CYNTHIA GARCIA

've realized that my favorite traditions are the ones that happen naturally, the ones we don't set out to create but that develop over time. Our family has many traditions, but they're simple ones, like making and eating food together, settling in to watch holiday movies, and enjoying something sweet and warm.

Each winter we make arroz con leche (rice with milk), which requires just a few ingredients that we always have on hand. We enjoy this wonderful treat together and then head back to the couch for more movies and sweet memories. It's a simple tradition but one our family loves.

 SAFETY TIP

Using the stove can be dangerous and should be done with adult supervision.

INGREDIENTS

6 cups milk

6 cups water

¾ cup rice

1½ cups sugar

Pinch of salt

1 cinnamon stick

INSTRUCTIONS

1. Pour the water, rice, sugar, salt, and cinnamon into a pot and simmer on the stovetop on high heat until the rice is fully cooked (16 to 18 minutes).

2. Once the rice is cooked, add in the milk.

3. Wait for it to boil and it's done.

4. Pour into your favorite mugs and add a cinnamon stick if you'd like. Enjoy.

What are the foods or drinks that your family considers traditions? What tastes conjure up the holiday season for you and your children?

NATURE-STAMPED ORNAMENTS

My favorite ornaments to unbox are the ones my children have made over the years. From the beautiful wool-felted creations and delicate works of art to the lopsided candy canes and gingerbread men with crooked smiles, every ornament one of my children has handmade holds special memories from years past. Making ornaments together is one of our favorite traditions, and we look forward to it every year.

This year, we made nature-stamped ornaments that use inexpensive ingredients and require no baking. We used a variety of plants, stamps, and cookie presses to make the impressions on our ornaments. Once you make your dough, the possibilities of what you can create are endless. Enjoy making a lovely mess with your kids. The results will be well worth it. (This activity will need adult participation and supervision.)

MATERIALS

2 cups baking soda

1 cup cornstarch

1¼ cups cool water

A pot

Spoon for mixing

Parchment paper

Rolling pin

Cookie cutters

Leaves, plants, nature finds

Chopstick, straw, or small dowel

Twine or ribbon

 SAFETY TIP

Using the stove can be dangerous and should be done with adult supervision.

INSTRUCTIONS

1. Pour cornstarch, baking soda, and water into a medium-size pot and, with a spoon, stir all ingredients together until they are well mixed. The consistency should be runny.

2. Once the ingredients are mixed together, place the pot on the stove over medium heat and stir continuously. The mixture will begin to thicken. Make sure to keep stirring so that the dough thickens evenly and doesn't burn.

3. As soon as the mixture becomes solid and there is no liquid left, remove from heat. At this point, you should have a ball of soft and pliable dough

4. The dough will be very hot and will need to be handled carefully. Remove dough from pot with a large spoon and place it in a large bowl.

5. Cover the bowl with damp paper towels and allow the dough to cool until it is cool enough to handle. It is very important to use the damp paper towels as they will help keep your dough from drying out.

6. Once your dough has cooled enough to handle, take some and knead it. (It's important to only roll and cut small portions of

dough at a time, otherwise the dough can dry out. Working with only enough dough to make two or three ornaments at a time and leaving the rest in the bowl covered in damp paper towels, to keep the dough soft and pliable, is best.) Your dough will become nice and smooth. Roll it into a ball, and place it on a hard, even surface covered with parchment paper. Using the rolling pin, roll your dough out to approximately ¼-inch thickness. If your dough sticks to your rolling pin, you can sprinkle a little cornstarch on it.

7. Use your cookie cutters to cut out your desired shapes.

8. Once you have your shapes cut out, take your leaves and plants and press them into the dough. You will want to press them in gently but deep enough so that they leave a good impression.

9. Gently lift up and remove your leaves.

10. With the end of a chopstick, make a small hole at the top of the ornament for hanging. A straw or small dowel could also be used.

11. Allow ornaments to dry overnight, turning them over halfway through their drying time to ensure they dry evenly. Alternatively, you can bake the ornaments at 325°F for 30 minutes on a cookie sheet lined with parchment paper. Baking will brown the ornaments a bit, however, so if you prefer bright white ornaments the overnight drying process is best.

12. Once your ornaments are completely dry, add twine or ribbon for hanging. One full batch of the recipe will make 18 to 20 medium-size ornaments.

BY NAOMI OVANDO

CHRISTMAS COOKIES
AS HANDCRAFTS

Each year I roll out sticky sugar cookie dough and help little hands press cookie cutters into the dough and carefully lay the shapes onto a baking sheet. We dry tears as reindeer antlers break off and celebrate achieving the perfect golden-brown tint as we pull a tray out of the oven.

I'm sharing my mom's beloved sugar cookie recipe here and wishing you all a lovely holiday season as you create alongside your children.

Remember that when little hands (and the rest of your kitchen) are covered in sticky dough and colored icing, you are doing so much more than *just* making cookies. Your family's cookie baking is helping to develop the wonderful and exquisite instruments of your children's hands and minds, not to mention a loving tradition they will carry in their hearts for many years.

 SAFETY TIP

Using the oven can be dangerous and should be done with adult supervision.

TIPS FOR MAKING SUGAR COOKIES

- Don't rush. You can plan for this to be an all-day project. I try to complete the steps at separate intervals and let my children play elsewhere while I prep for them. To start, I gather all the supplies and then call the children to help me mix up the dough.

- As I chill the dough, I prep the kitchen for cutting out the cookies. I call in each child one at a time to cut out as many cookies as they would like, and when everyone has had their fill, I finish the rest.

- As the cookies bake, I put a tablecloth on our dining room table and fill separate bowls with icing, sprinkles, candies, etc. Once the cookies are baked and cooled, we gather around the dining room table to listen to Christmas music and decorate.

- As the cookies are iced, we lay the finished ones back on the baking trays until the icing dries. Then I put them in lidded containers with wax paper between each layer of cookies.

SUGAR COOKIES

YIELD: MAKES 2 DOZEN

⅔ cup shortening

¾ cup granulated sugar

1 teaspoon vanilla

1 egg

4 teaspoons milk

2 cups sifted all-purpose flour

1½ teaspoons baking powder

¼ teaspoon salt

ICING

3 cups powdered sugar

1 teaspoon vanilla

Tiny pinch of salt

2 tablespoons milk
(add more if too stiff)

1. Cream together shortening, sugar, and vanilla.

2. Add egg. Beat until light and fluffy. Stir in milk.

3. Sift together dry ingredients, then blend into creamed mixture.

4. Divide dough in half. Chill one hour.

5. On lightly floured surface, roll half of dough to ⅛-inch thickness. Keep the other half in the refrigerator until ready to use.

6. Cut into fun shapes with cookie cutters. If the dough you are working with becomes warm and sticky, place back in the fridge for a short time.

7. Bake on greased cookie sheets at 375°F for 6 to 8 minutes or until lightly browned on the bottom.

8. Allow cookies to cool for 5 minutes, then carefully move to wire racks.

9. Blend the icing ingredients together until smooth. A handheld mixer works well.

10. Ice the cookies with a knife and decorate with sprinkles and candy, while playing holiday music, of course!

BY SHARON MCKEEMAN

BOOK ADVENT

BY JAMIE WOLMA

When my children were tiny, I started collecting Christmas books, ones with profound storylines and rich vocabularies, to prepare our hearts for the holiday in the weeks leading up to it.

For the first few years, I merely piled books in a basket under the tree, many of them board books for little hands. But as my children have grown older, we've started wrapping them—one for each night of December until Christmas Eve.

Now that my older two are big enough to help with the wrapping, we've made a tradition out of our "Book Advent" preparation. We began this year by baking homemade cookies in the kitchen and setting the table with package embellishments and kraft paper for the wrapping.

The table was a mess of candlelight, homemade cookies, pinecones we'd gathered in the yard, potato stamps we'd made while our cookies baked, stamp pads, cranberries and oranges we had dried the previous night, string and twine, and our stacks of books. We played Christmas music and took frequent breaks for dancing and snacking and discussions about Christmas.

When our twenty-four packages were fully wrapped and adorned with whatever my children saw fit, we stacked them neatly into a wooden wagon and placed it next to the woodstove.

Each day I glance over at that wagon full of Christmas books wrapped up in the sweetest handmade wrappings and daydream about our Advent season, marked by nights by the fire, just us unwrapping those books and reading together, with lighted candles and bellies full of warm cocoa, each story bringing us closer to the greatest story of all time.

_____

What are your family's favorite Christmas books? Do you have any traditions around reading them together?

_____

HOLIDAY
CROWNS

n our house, it's a rule that if it can be bent into a circle and worn, rest assured, I will fashion it into a crown and let the kids wear it until it falls apart. We wear tinsel, live flowers, fake flowers, ornaments, trinkets, paper, pipe cleaners—you get the idea.

Crowns can elevate any outfit from cozy to over-the-top holiday wear in an instant.

They also can serve as the perfect party accessory. Make a crown and snap some portraits. Better yet, get out those pipe cleaners and let your crew make them! Give them away as party favors or stack them on your prettiest presents as an extra gift from the heart.

You can walk out into your backyard and grab the necessary materials. Stop along the roadside, buy some grocery store flowers, carve time to wander in a forest or field. The world is your craft store!

MATERIALS

Scissors

Floral wire/tape (or hot glue gun)

Natural coiled wire

Crown materials (fabric headband, natural items like flowers, leaves, small branches, berries, or items from a craft store, like small pine trees, bells, and figurines shown here—get creative!)

🧰 SAFETY TIP

Hot glue and scissors can be dangerous and should be used with adult supervision.

INSTRUCTIONS

1. Measure your crown wearer's head with the coiled wire (allow for some give and shaping after placement), and then create the pattern you are hoping to achieve, securing it with floral wire or hot glue. For the pine and berry example, I snipped a few healthy pieces of pine and common winterberry with scissors for a classic red and green look.

2. Assemble your crown. This will take some trial and error; you will probably have to make more than one. The assembling process may frustrate you, and that's okay. There is no such thing as right or wrong or too much or too little. Layer, fill, and add as you see fit. Think fondly of Carmen Miranda's fruit numbers and be inspired to go big.

3. Holiday crowns are all about art and expression, unique to you and the little souls you are sharing with. The only way to do it wrong is if they don't make you feel like you just stepped out of Narnia.

BY SUZI KERN

MISTLETOE KISSING BALL

No matter what your traditions are around the holidays, the most meaningful ones bring you closer together. Such is the "mistletoe kissing ball" for our family. Around the first part of December, the kids and I bundle up and go outside to trim boxwood clippings from our bushes and nearby evergreens.

We get excited as we bring the clippings into the house and with them, the first sweet smells of Christmas. The kids hover over my shoulder as I piece together each clipping. After I hang it, the fun begins.

For the next weeks, as I'm doing housework, I'll hear, "I'm under the mistletooooeeee!" Sweet little babes, waiting to be peppered with kisses. They'll laugh, and I'll know that getting my hands sticky with sap is worth this priceless tradition. May your kisses be plentiful!

MATERIALS

Garden shears

Baseball-size foam ball (porous is better)

Green clippings (I use boxwood and several evergreens from around my home)

Scissors

Thick wire or a metal hanger

Wire pliers

Your choice of ribbon

Berries (real ones if you can forage; if not, fake are fine)

Optional: hot glue gun

 SAFETY TIP

Garden shears, scissors, and hot glue can be dangerous and should be used with adult supervision.

INSTRUCTIONS

1. Forage green clippings that are about 6 to 8 inches long with garden shears. Make sure they are fairly dry but not completely dried out and dead.

2. Use scissors to poke holes into the Styrofoam ball and insert clippings all over the ball.

3. If you're concerned about the clippings staying firmly in place, give each one just a dab with the hot glue.

4. Once the ball is completely covered with clippings, add in the berries. This might help cover any white spots you still may see.

5. Fashion a wire hook. You can use thick wire or cut off the hook end of a wire hanger. Twist it with pliers to make a loop but leave a long end to insert into the ball. This may require a dab of glue, too, depending on how heavy your ball is.

6. Decide where the top of the ball is and stick the long end of your hook in it. Use ribbon to create a hanging loop through the hook. Then hang your kissing ball in a location in your home where there's lots of foot traffic.

7. Enjoy the smooches!

BY LEA WU

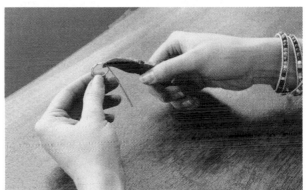

HOMEMADE ADVENT CALENDAR

For the past few years, I have been making Advent calendars to help us count down the days until Christmas. Our Advent calendar has a package or envelope for each day, and they contain a variety of things, from little gifts to ideas for special activities we can do together.

Each morning, we read a different chapter or picture book about Christmas and then the girls take turns opening a package or envelope. It's a wonderful tradition that all of us look forward to. Here's how you can make one with your family:

MATERIALS

Tape

Scissors

Twine

Cards and envelopes

Gifts

A hearty stick or piece of driftwood (about 3 feet long)

Wrapping paper

Ribbon or decorations (even flowers)

SAFETY TIP

Scissors can be dangerous and should be used with adult supervision.

INSTRUCTIONS

1. Gather 24 little gifts and/or activity cards, one for each day of Advent. I try to collect gifts for our calendar throughout the months leading up to Advent, including treats to eat, little items for their dollhouse, clay, toy animals, lip balm, and more. We also write special activities on cards, such as "Go get hot chocolate" and "Look at Christmas lights." You could also write "Game night," "Christmas caroling," or "Go to a Christmas play."

2. Using scissors and tape, wrap each gift or stuff each envelope. I prefer a more natural look, so I use brown paper grocery bags or plain brown wrapping paper. I add a little touch of ribbon or lace or flowers to some but not all of the presents. The calendar is up all month, so I try to keep it minimal but lovely.

3. Hammer a single nail into the wall and hang the stick with a piece of twine.

4. Lay all 24 gifts and envelopes out on the floor and decide where you want each item to hang from the stick. Then tie each one with twine to the stick.

5. Once everything is hung from the stick, write the day numbers on the gifts, not 1 to 24 from left to right, but in a more random order that will distribute the weight evenly along the stick as they are opened.

6. Each morning, your children can grab that day's package and open the gift together, counting down the days until your Christmas celebration.

BY KRISTIN ROGERS

HANDMADE WRAPPING PAPER

O ver the last several years, our family has made an effort to make holiday gift giving increasingly simple and meaningful. We want the focus of the season to be on the things that really matter, rather than the material and commercial aspects.

As a result, many of the gifts we give are homemade or have special meaning beyond their material value. The spirit in which a gift is given means so much more than the item itself, and we want to pass that truth on to our kids.

Putting special care into the presentation of gifts is a wonderful way to communicate the love with which each one is being given, and that doesn't mean spending a lot of money on fancy gift wrap.

A few years ago, I began wrapping most of the gifts I give in simple brown kraft paper decorated by my kids and me. We save all the brown shipping paper that comes stuffed in packages we get throughout the year (the creases and imperfections just add to the charm), and sometimes purchase rolls of it if we need more.

I've also cut up paper grocery bags to use for smaller gifts. Then my kids get to have fun decorating the paper with stamps and paint, and finish with items they find in nature. No two are alike, and none is perfect, but they each reflect our family and make for a truly special gift.

MATERIALS

Brown kraft paper (can buy at a craft store or online, or reuse brown grocery bags)

Scissors

Rubber stamps and ink pads

Pencils with erasers

Paint and paintbrushes

Items found in nature, such as pinecones, flowers, feathers, etc.

 SAFETY TIP

Scissors can be dangerous and should be used with adult supervision.

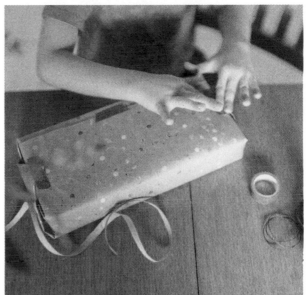

INSTRUCTIONS

1. Tear or cut paper into the appropriate size for the gift to be wrapped.

2. Stamp or paint the entire surface of the sheet of paper—there are so many pretty rubber stamps at craft supply stores, and pencil erasers make excellent polka-dot stamps. Sometimes I'll just let the kids go crazy with colorful paint.

3. Gather items from nature (sticks, feathers, pinecones, flowers, etc.) to add finishing touches. Sometimes my older son will paint those as well.

BY HANNAH MAYO

THE LION, THE WITCH, AND THE WARDROBE

BY HANNAH WESTBELD

Every year, on the first of December, we pull our beloved copy of C. S. Lewis's *The Lion, the Witch, and the Wardrobe* from its reserved spot on our bookshelf and embark on an adventure into the magical world of Narnia. For our family, it's a tradition as constant as the decorating of our Christmas tree and the opening of our Advent doors.

For our first official reading of the year, we gather oranges and cloves for pomanders, pop popcorn, and gather cranberries for stringing a garland. As our busy hands work and the sweet and spicy smells of oranges and cloves blend together with the sound of my silly British accent, the story pours over us and the pages fly by.

Over the course of the month, as we savor each turned page, my children don costumes, draw swords, and are inspired to engage in imaginative play, battling against evil and fighting together for Aslan.

Somehow, as the years pass and our children grow older, the story continues to grow in depth right along with them, the message conveyed through story embedding itself deeper and deeper into their hearts and minds. It is a message of relentless grace and courage and of a peace and goodness worth fighting for. And, through Edmund, a reminder that no matter how far we may stray from goodness, true and abiding love meets us with grace, welcome, and acceptance.

It's a message my husband and I hope will continue to steady the hearts of our children long after they've left the haven of our home. So no matter where they go, no matter how far, they'll have that surety to carry with them every day of their lives.

And maybe one Christmas, many years from now, they'll think of Aslan, and of Peter, Susan, Edmund, and Lucy, and they'll be transported to a moment in time when my voice and the warmth of my arms wrapped them in the love and peace of a beautiful adventure.

What story transports you back to your childhood? What is your favorite story to read to your children? What message do you hope it conveys to them?

STORYBOOK ORNAMENTS

Each year, my mother-in-law creates a new set of ornaments for her Christmas tree. She has handcrafted felt birds, hearts, yarn balls, and storybook ornaments out of book pages. For the storybook ornaments, after removing memorable sections of book pages, she cuts the paper into strips and glues them onto an ornament using Mod Podge.

Our shared passion for reading and ornaments inspired me to make my own.

For my ornaments, I chose pages from old hymnals that my mom picked up from a garage sale. Selecting hymns and discussing each song with my children was my favorite part of this project. This would work just as well with pages from favorite books (that you don't mind tearing pages from!) as well.

Not all ornaments are made to hang unnoticed on the tree and collect dust. Let us gather with our families and create heirlooms that lead to deep conversations, bond us together, and nurture new traditions to be passed down for years.

MATERIALS

Plastic ornaments (old ornaments you have on hand or from the dollar store)

Book(s) of choice

Mod Podge

Scissors

Sponge paintbrush

Ribbon or twine

Optional: greenery and/or dried cranberries

SAFETY TIP

Scissors can be dangerous and should be used with adult supervision.

INSTRUCTIONS

1. Use scissors to cut pages from a book into thin strips.

2. With sponge paintbrush, paint Mod Podge onto the ornament.

3. Place book strips vertically on the ornament.

4. Paint Mod Podge over strips.

5. Allow to dry and hang with twine or ribbon.

6. Tie optional greenery and cranberries into twine.

BY CAROL ANN SARTELL

RUSTIC WOVEN
WINTER STARS

It grows colder here. Soon we will notice Old Man Winter circling the corners of our crooked farmhouse, stomping his white boots on the threshold, rapping his icy knuckles against the windowpanes.

The cold and wet have never kept my three boys indoors for too long, as they prefer to be cocooned in their warm woolens and sent out for long hours to romp and dig and poke at the lacy veins of ice that splinter across our pond.

These natural rhythms are steadfast and familiar to us. Yet each year the earnestness of energetic outdoor exploration gradually begins to surrender to a slower rhythm of winter's quiet light and the deeply inward focus of body and mind so valued this time of year by those of us who live in colder climates.

Keeping little hands busy with daily projects and handcrafts has always been my favorite way to bring meaningful work to this season of coziness within the home. We dip candles, string lights, dance to scratchy vinyl records, practice our knitting, and weave hanging stars to prepare for the beautiful winter darkness.

And the best part is that I can encourage my children to practice thoughtful generosity with their creations through the holidays and to learn how much recipients value simple, slowly handmade things.

MATERIALS

Cardboard scraps with two smooth sides and a corrugated center

Pieces of scrap paper, fabric, or natural treasures (We used old book pages, lace, and pieces of birch bark, but be creative with what you might want to use: Vintage illustrations? Stamps? Photos? Washi tape? Pressed flowers or leaves? Dried moss? Seashells or acorn caps? There are so many options that would look lovely with this project!)

Thin twine or yarn

Straight pins

Double-sided tape or glue

Scissors

Measuring tape

Optional: needle and thread for hanging

Scissors and needles can be dangerous and should be used with adult supervision.

INSTRUCTIONS

1. Use the measuring tape and scissors to cut two equal squares of corrugated cardboard to your desired size. Then cut two pieces of your chosen scrap paper/fabric to identical dimensions or a bit smaller than the cardboard squares. We chose 2 inches by 2 inches.

2. Tape/glue your two pieces of cardboard together, rotating the bottom piece to form the base shape of the star (all eight corners should be visible) and adhere one of your paper scraps to the top.

3. Flip your star over and lay the end of your ball of twine in the center of the backside. Adhere the second piece of cut paper to the cardboard, fixing the twine into place. (We found the double-stick tape to work best for this purpose, but if you are using glue you will need to wait for it to dry before moving on to the next steps.)

4. Select eight straight pins and carefully secure them into each of the eight corners,

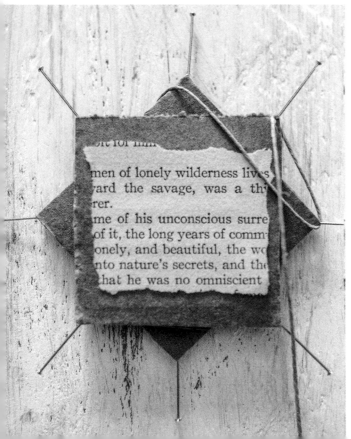

through the corrugated part between the two outer layers of cardboard. They should be snugly sandwiched with about one-third of the pin in the cardboard. Make sure there are no sharp tips poking out anywhere in the star's middle!

5. Starting at the topmost pin, begin your weaving clockwise around the star by following the pattern of "two pins down, one pin up." This means you will lift your twine from the first pin down around the third pin (skipping over the second), and then back up around the second pin.

9. Continue wrapping consecutive layers around the star in this manner, slowly moving inward to the center of the star as you wrap each layer to the left of the previous round, until the cardboard spaces are completely covered, and the delicate woven pattern has emerged!

10. When you decide that your star is complete, cut the twine and conceal its end by knotting it through one of the strings on the backside of the star.

11. Very gently push each of the straight pins all the way into the star, again making sure that there are no sharp tips poking out. Each pin should be nestled hidden in the cardboard's corrugated interior.

12. If you desire to hang your handiwork, use a needle to string a length of thread through the topmost corner of the star. The 2-inch by 2-inch size we created for this tutorial is a standard ornament or gift-tag size and looks lovely hung on a seasonal wreath or multiplied to create a winter garland. A much larger star would certainly look striking as a tree topper or on a winter nature shelf.

BY LEAH DAMON

6. After circling the second pin, lift your twine down around the fourth pin (this time skipping the third) and then come back up and around the third pin.

7. Continue this pattern of "two pins down, one pin up" until you have wrapped one layer around the entire star. We found that it helps to slowly turn the star in one hand as you wrap around it with the other.

8. Begin your second layer using the same pattern, but this time as you wrap, lay each piece of twine parallel but slightly to the left of the one you wrapped around the first time.

PAPER
STARS

My children and I enjoy making paper stars to hang in our windows for the rich colors they bring during a bleak and gray season. What we love best is when the light streaming through the window instantly transforms the stars. Suddenly, their various geometric patterns and overlapping colors come together like the reflections inside a kaleidoscope, just waiting to be discovered.

MATERIALS

Kite paper

Ruler

Scissors

Glue stick

 SAFETY TIP

Scissors can be dangerous and should be used with adult supervision.

TIPS FOR MAKING PAPER STARS

- Take care with your folds to be sure that the points and edges match exactly. The folding must be precise in order for the star to reveal those beautiful geometric patterns we desire.

- After you line up each edge and point carefully, press each crease well with your finger.

- In the steps that require glue, use a light layer of glue with a glue stick. Using a glue bottle resulted in a crinkling of the kite paper and a less pleasing end result. Using too much glue from the glue stick left a purple residue inside the star.

- When you finish your star, press it flat by carefully placing heavy books on top of it.

- Experiment with various sizes for this project. We enjoyed making stars both large and small. The suggested dimensions are just a starting place.

- Likewise, feel free to experiment with a variety of colors too. Our favorite stars had various colors within a single star or an ombre effect. Get creative!

SIMPLE EIGHT-POINT STAR

INSTRUCTIONS

1. Use a ruler and scissors to carefully cut out eight 3 × 3-inch squares of kite paper.

2. Take one square and fold it in half diagonally. Then press along the crease with your finger.

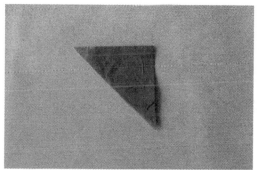

3. Open up the square and fold one edge toward the center crease so that the edge is aligned with the center crease.

4. Repeat to the other side. This will form a classic kite shape.

5. Using a glue stick and only a thin layer of glue, glue the flaps down.

6. Repeat with the remaining seven squares.

ASSEMBLE THE STAR

1. With the flap side facing down, line up the left bottom edge of the right point to the center crease of the point on the left, matching the bottom points. Glue in place.

2. Continue to assemble the rest of the points in this way, moving clockwise.

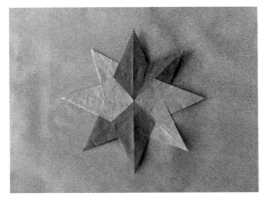

(*Simple Eight-Point Star continued*)

3. After you glue on the eighth point, lift up the left side of the first point and glue it on top of the right side of the eighth point.

4. Press your completed star flat. Then adhere it to your window with a bit of clear tape.

SIMPLE TEN-POINT STAR

INSTRUCTIONS

1. Create this star in the same way as you made the simple eight-point star but use

(*Simple Ten-Point Star continued*)

ten squares instead of eight to create ten points.

ASSEMBLE THE STAR

1. Rather than line the left edge of the right point with the center crease of the left point like you did with the eight-point star, you will instead bring the left edge of the right point just beyond the center crease. You will still match the bottom points of each point at the center of the star. Make sure the flap side of each point is facing down as you assemble the star.

2. After you glue on the tenth point, lift up the left side of the point and glue it on top of the right side of the tenth point.

3. After pressing flat, adhere to your window using a piece of clear tape.

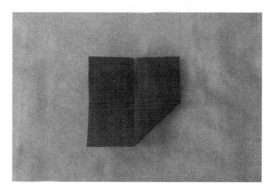

LARGE EIGHT-POINT STAR

INSTRUCTIONS

1. Start with eight 6 × 6-inch squares.

2. Fold the square in half lengthwise. Press the crease with your finger. Open the square and fold it in half widthwise. Press the crease again. When you open up your square, you will see four equal quadrants.

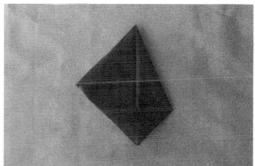

3. Starting at one quadrant, press the corner point up to the center point, forming a triangle. Repeat to the other three quadrants.

4. Turn the square so the center crease runs vertically and the square looks like a diamond. Fold the right point down so the edge is aligned with the center crease.

5. Repeat to the other side, folding the left point down so the edge is aligned with the center crease.

6. You will now have a classic kite shape.

7. Lightly glue the flaps in place.

8. Repeat with the other seven squares.

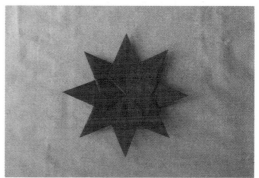

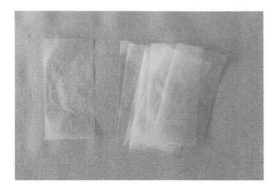

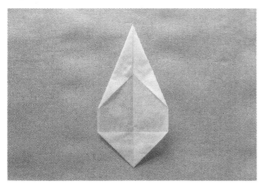

(Large Eight-Point Star continued)

ASSEMBLE THE STAR

1. With the flap side facing down, line up the left bottom edge of the right point with the center crease of the point on the left, matching the bottom points. Glue in place.

2. Continue to assemble the rest of the points in this way, moving clockwise.

3. After you glue on the eighth point, lift up the left side of the first point and glue it on top of the right side of the eighth point.

4. After pressing your star flat, adhere the star to your window with a piece of clear tape.

FANCY EIGHT-POINT STAR

INSTRUCTIONS

1. Cut out eight 3 × 6-inch rectangles.

2. Fold the first rectangle in half lengthwise, being sure the edges and corners line up exactly. Press the crease well.

3. Open up the rectangle. Fold the bottom corners up to meet the center crease, forming two small triangles.

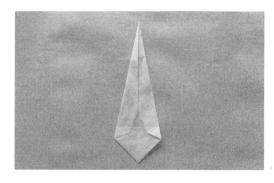

(Fancy Eight-Point Star continued)

4. Repeat to the top corners.

5. Fold the right point of the top right triangle in to meet the center crease, so the right edge of the triangle lines up perfectly along the center crease.

6. Repeat to the left side, bringing the left point and edge to the center crease.

7. Fold the right side in one final time, bringing the far-right point in to meet the center crease. Line up the right edge perfectly along the center crease and press the crease well.

8. Repeat to the left side, bringing the left point and edge to the center crease.

9. Using a light layer of glue, glue the flaps down so that they lie flat.

ASSEMBLE THE STAR

1. With the flap side facing down, line up the left bottom edge of the right point along the center crease of the point on the left. Glue in place.

2. Continue to assemble the rest of the points in this way, moving clockwise.

3. After you glue on the eighth point, lift the left side of the first point and glue it on top of the right side of the eighth point.

4. After pressing flat, adhere the star to your window using a piece of clear tape on the back of the star.

BY RACHEL KOVAC

THE PROMISE OF A NEW YEAR

BY AINSLEY ARMENT

What is this mystery that marks a new year? The clock turns and we begin anew. The sun rises on the universe like the dawning of a new world. And I can't help but think that the magic of time is either hollow or holy, because it is what we make of it.

The miracle of a new year lies not in our ability to mark it with resolutions but our vision to see the possibilities it holds. The eighteenth-century writer Jonathan Swift wrote, "Vision is the art of seeing what is invisible to others."

Ten years ago, I envisioned a different life for my son—one outside the box of classrooms, report cards, and roll calls. I saw snapshots of a wild and free childhood, of family adventures, and of interest-led learning. I didn't make a master plan or fill a calendar with goals to conquer. But I allowed my vision to carry me forth into the unknown. Each year has been a wild adventure, full of beauty and goodness, mishaps and mistakes.

It takes vision to live wild and free. To live a life divergent. Without vision, we would certainly stick with convention and simply plug into the program.

But you and I have seen a picture of the future that stirs our passions. We don't know what the path will hold, but we know the story will be worth telling someday.

Vision isn't a pull toward perfection but a pursuit of passion.

It isn't a promise of success but permission to make mistakes.

The magic of a new year is the gift of freedom to try new things, let go of rigid resolutions, and rediscover our vision for this lifestyle. So set your course accordingly and brace yourself, dear friend, because a vision worth following is not a safe one.

As Helen Keller said, "Life is either a daring adventure or nothing at all."

MIDWINTER LANTERNS

'm always excited about winter when the season is bright and new—the morning frost coating autumn's fallen leaves, the first snow, and cozy afternoons by the fire, reading (and endlessly rereading) all our favorite winter books. Soon enough, the holidays follow, candle-lit and cinnamon-scented. And while we gather close to celebrate the darkest days of the year, we also joyfully acknowledge the birth of a new light.

But as the weeks wear on, winter deepens and starts to lose its sparkle. The Christmas tree is taken outside to be planted in the woods, the decorations are carefully wrapped in their worn and wrinkled pieces of silk paper and packed away in boxes for another year to come. And then one day we notice that all the colors are gone. The slopes around the house are barren and brown, and even though we know that the sun has already started climbing again, inevitably journeying toward her summer zenith, there is always a moment that the dark starts to feel heavy and long.

This is the moment when I start longing for spring.

But then I am reminded of the story of the poet mouse *Frederick* by Leo Lionni, a beautiful storybook my boys love so very much. All summer long, little Frederick seems to do nothing but daydream, basking in the golden sun, while the other mice prepare for winter by gathering food.

Annoyed by his apparent laziness, the mice ask Frederick why he's not working like them. He answers that he's busy gathering the warm rays of the sun, the bright colors of summer, and all the beautiful words. So when winter comes, and the mice grow hungry and cold in their cozy den, he lifts their spirits and warms their hearts with poetry.

And so we gather around the table with our craft supplies, to spend a day together, making a set of midwinter lanterns to light our dark evenings and to lift our spirits too.

MATERIALS

Reclaimed wood or plywood

8 straight willow branches of even thickness (8 to 10 inches)

Optional: 1 longer willow branch for a handle (14 to 16 inches)

Compass with pencil

4 nails

Hot glue (or white glue)

Silk paper

LED tealight

Sandpaper

An old paintbrush for the glue

Scissors

Hand drill, with a drill bit that approximately matches the thickness of your sticks

A hammer

A small bow saw (or electric saw)

 SAFETY TIP

Using drills, saws, scissors, and hot glue can be dangerous and should be used with adult supervision.

INSTRUCTIONS

1. With the compass, draw two identical circles onto your wood panels.

2. Draw a second, smaller circle inside one of the circles, leaving at least a 1-inch margin. This will be your top circle.

3. Measure out where you are going to place the sticks that will connect the top and bottom—eight at equal intervals—and mark the spots on the bottom and top circles.

4. Place the LED tealight you're planning to use in the center of the bottom circle and trace around it. Then hammer four nails around the perimeter to keep the tealight in place.

5. Carefully drill the holes you previously marked on your circles.

   a. Don't drill all the way through the bottom circle—just enough to make the sticks fit in.

   b. Take the top circle and drill all the way through two of the holes on opposite sides of the circle.

6. Using the (bow) saw, carefully cut the circles out of the wood panel.

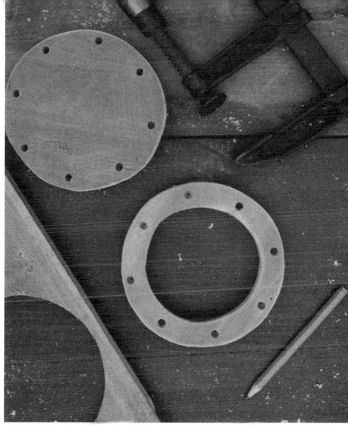

7. Sand both pieces until all the edges are smooth.

8. Prepare the willow branches:

    a. If you're planning to give the lantern a handle, prepare eight sticks of exactly the same length, and leave one longer one.

    b. If you're making a lantern without a handle, prepare all the sticks to be the same length.

9. Place the sticks into the holes you drilled in the bottom circle and glue them into place.

10. Fit the sticks into the top circle and glue them in place.

11. For the handle, carefully bend the long willow branch into a U shape. Pass it through both the holes you drilled all the way through the top circle and glue into the holes in the bottom circle.

12. With scissors, cut a strip of silk paper that will fit the height and the circumference of your lantern, leaving some margin.

13. Use paintbrush to apply a thin layer of glue on the outside of the sticks.

14. Glue the paper onto the structure. The easiest way to do this is by starting at one of the sticks. Carefully smooth the beginning of your paper strip around the stick a bit, so it has some overlap. Then stretch the paper over the rest of the lamp.

15. Check to be sure everything looks nice and smooth, cut away the margin, and glue.

Now your lamp is ready to shine!

Of course, you can decorate your midwinter lanterns by carefully gluing papercuts, paper doilies, dried flowers, or leaves onto the inside of the silk paper. The possibilities are endless. Each and every one will be full of magic and poetry, just like little Frederick's words in the deepest, darkest days of winter.

BY KATRIEN VAN DEUREN

MINDFUL LOVE BASKETS

There is no expression more intimate than a love letter. I don't only mean the romantic ones. I mean the love letters that make a person feel genuinely seen and deeply cherished—even if the words are humble and the delivery falls short of poetry.

A painting can be a love letter, or a little mason jar of wildflowers left quietly on the windowsill from my husband on a day when he understands that my spirit is weary. Even the very first flowers my sons ever picked for me—crushed in sweaty palms but brandished with pride—spoke more love to my sentimental heart than any card or packaged chocolate.

This year, in place of the usual Valentine's cards and sweets, our family is beginning a new tradition of "handmade love baskets."

During the first days of February leading up to St. Valentine's Day, each of us will drop a simple but meaningful secret note, doodle, or nature gift into each of the baskets that belong to the other family members. Then, on the morning of the fourteenth, each family member will finally be able to peek inside his or her own basket

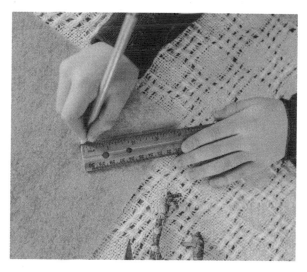

and enjoy the encouragement that comes from reading the collection of love letters.

Gifts are simple and natural: little items such as shells, gemstones, painted rocks, origami, dried flowers, or drawings are excellent contributions that even prewriters can gather or create. This process fosters intentional generosity in even the littlest family members as they are on the lookout for items they know a particular parent or sibling might enjoy. Older children may appreciate small school or art supplies such as fun paper clips or washi tape.

But whatever you choose to fill your baskets with, make sure you take the time to be simple and intentional about the personal nature of your treasures and your words.

MATERIALS

12 × 12-inch square of sturdy felt

Ruler

Pencil

Scissors

2 clothespins

Twine or strong string/yarn

Two small sticks, 3 to 4 inches in length

Dried nature elements

Glue gun

Scrap lace or fabric (to line the basket interior)

Bits and pieces of charming scrap papers for writing notes

 SAFETY TIP

Hot glue and scissors can be dangerous and should be used with adult supervision.

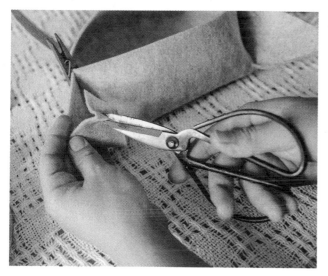

INSTRUCTIONS

1. Using a pencil and ruler, draw a 4-inch diagonal line from each corner to the center of your felt square.

2. Use scissors to cut along each of the four pencil lines.

3. Starting on the side of the felt square that is closest to you, pull together the left and right corners so their top edges align. You are creating the inner layer of your basket.

4. Clamp these pieces together with a clothespin and repeat with the opposite corners on the side of the felt that is farthest from you. (Once the outside layer of felt has later been secured, you can come back and readjust these inner corners to tighten or loosen if necessary.)

5. Use scissors to cut small, ¼- to ½-inch slits inside each of the four remaining felt corners. Turn the basket so that the two sides with the clothespins are positioned on your left and right. (The remaining corners will fold up to overlap against the flat sides of the interior layer to create the "front" and "back" of the basket.)

6. Cut a long piece of twine and thread the two ends through the corner slits. Pull gently together to tighten the corners and secure with a knot, then wrap the remaining twine around one of your twigs to hold it in place and tie another knot or bow before trimming the excess to a length of your liking. Repeat on the other side of the basket to secure the last two corners.

7. Finally, remove the clothespins and re-adjust the inner corners if necessary, adding a small bead of hot glue between the layers to keep them from any future movement. A hot glue gun can also be used to add a few dried nature elements to the front of your basket for a bit of whimsy.

8. If you wish, add a small scrap of lace or other fabric to line the interior of your basket before you begin to fill it with your precious gifts and words of love!

BY LEAH DAMON

WILDFLOWER
VALENTINES

In the last few years, I have made it my personal mission to restore our yard to a state that will support native flora and fauna. In cities and suburbs across our country, the local flora has been stripped away and replaced with ornamental, nonnative plants and trees.

This process, unseen to most people, has impacted the local ecosystem. Nonnative plants do not provide the sustenance that native animals need to survive, and they move to where they are able to find food, oftentimes leading to animals being hurt or relocated for pest control.

We found a way to save paper from the garbage bin with this fun project, recycling it into a beautiful gift to give while also spreading the love with some native wildflower seeds.

MATERIALS

Source paper (Newspaper works great. Be sure to avoid any paper with a "glossy" finish as the coating will not break down in the decomposition and sprouting process.)

Native wildflower seeds (Talk with your local expert gardener or gardening group for the best place to source native seeds.)

Optional: paper shredder

Mixing bowls

Blender

Mesh tray (We used a simple mesh tray that you would use to pan for precious stones—mesh over a rectangle made with 2 × 4s. You can use any sort of mesh placed on top of a cookie sheet or pan to collect water.)

Shallow pan or cookie sheet

Optional: rolling pin

Optional: extra newspaper (for blotting)

Optional: hair dryer

 SAFETY TIP

Using a blender or paper shredder can be dangerous and should be done with adult supervision.

INSTRUCTIONS

1. A day or so ahead of time, use a paper shredder to shred your source paper or have your kids work on tearing up the paper into smaller pieces. (I turned my kids loose on our kitchen floor with a stack of paper from recycling and some newspapers, along with some shredded paper from a recent package I had ordered. It was so much fun!)

2. On the day you're ready to work, gather a large mixing bowl, a blender, the seeds, the shallow pan, screen or mesh, and your raw material paper.

3. Place the shredded paper in the blender with water. (I filled our blender to the max line with paper and added 1 cup of water. It turned out to not be enough, so I added a bit more.)

4. Use the "pulse" option on your blender to pulverize the paper and turn it into a pulp. You want your pulp to be very thick, like hearty mashed potatoes.

5. Once your pulp is ready, remove it from the blender with a long spoon and place it into a large mixing bowl.

6. Add your wildflower seeds to the pulp in the large mixing bowl. It is VERY important that you do not add the seeds to the blender, as it will pulverize your seeds and they will not grow.

7. Let your kids get their hands dirty and gently squeeze and mix the seeds into the paper pulp. (This is a fun, sensory play activity that serves a great purpose!)

8. Once the seeds are mixed well, get your screen or mesh ready. Place the pan or cookie sheet under it to catch the excess water.

9. Place the pulp on the screen in large scoops.

10. Using your hands, gently press the pulp into the screen to create an even layer. Be careful that your pulp does not touch the sides of the screen if it has a wood border because it will be harder to remove later.

11. Continue gently pressing, or using a rolling pin, until your pulp is a narrow layer on your screen.

12. Allow the pulp to dry for a while (up to a day or two), checking it often. You can also use pieces of newspaper and a paper towel, pressed gently over your pulp layer, to help remove water. Be sure to remove the newspaper immediately after pressing, or your pulp will dry and bond to the newspaper. If your pulp is too thick, you can use a hair dryer on low to help speed up the drying process.

13. Once the paper is dry, gently remove your new seed paper from the screen or mesh.

14. Carefully tear or cut the seed paper into your desired shapes.

15. To give as valentines, cut into hearts or desired shapes. You can also use a hole puncher to put a small hole in the paper to tie a tag. On the tag write out the planting instructions.

PLANTING INSTRUCTIONS

1. Take the seed paper and place it into the ground (if it's above freezing). Cover with a shallow layer of dirt and give the seeds a little water.

2. If it is too cold to plant outside, place the seeds in a pot and cover with a shallow layer of dirt. Add water and place the pot in a sunny place.

3. The seeds will sprout in a few days, and you can enjoy watching them grow.

4. If you planted your wildflowers in a pot, you can transplant them outside once it warms up and observe them all spring and summer.

BY NICHOLE HOLZE

CUPID'S ARROW VALENTINES

Valentine's Day is a day to celebrate love, friendship, and kindness. My kids and I had fun making these homemade valentines for our friends. You could personalize them by adding color, using glitter heart stickers in lieu of felt ones, or by collecting sticks from your yard to replace the paper straws for a zero-waste option. The possibilities are endless. Play around with ideas and get messy!

MATERIALS

Scissors

Paper straws

Felt

Hot glue gun and glue or fabric glue

Twine

Feathers

Cardstock

Hole punch

Optional: washi tape

 SAFETY TIP

Scissors and hot glue can be dangerous and should be used with adult supervision.

INSTRUCTIONS

1. Start with three or four feathers and glue them into one end of a paper straw. (Hot glue works best because it dries quickly and keeps your feathers in place nicely. If the craft is going to be done completely unassisted, washi tape could be used to keep the feathers around the end of the straw.)

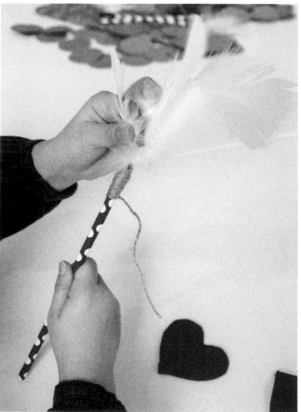

2. With the scissors, cut your felt into a heart shape. You'll need two for every arrow valentine. Glue a pair of felt hearts together, sandwiching your paper straw on the opposite end of the feathers, and let dry for a few minutes.

3. While your glue is setting, use the cardstock to make your tags.

4. Cut a 3-inch piece of twine and wrap it around the feathered end of your arrow, gluing a few spots as you go. Leave enough twine on the ends to dangle for the next step.

5. To put the finishing touches on your valentine, tie your tag to the tail of the twine.

6. Share your valentines with those you love.

BY SHANNON MOOERS

ROYAL
ICING
COOKIES

I f I could make one rule about sugar cookies (see page 86 for a recipe), it would be that they should always be iced. Royal icing is fun to use, and once you get the consistency right with a little time and patience, it's hard to stop piping creative and pretty designs onto a fresh batch of tasty cookies. And it's a great activity for your little ones!

When my girls join me in the kitchen for some baking, we all have more fun together, especially when I forgo my desire that everything be "perfect." I offer them frequent words of instruction and affirmation because, one day, when they are grown and look back at our time together, I want them to remember their childhood home as a place of shelter and acceptance. A place where they learned, but more importantly, a place where they were deeply loved.

So even when the project seems too advanced, I look for places where their little hands can help. The cookies may be misshapen and the icing designs simple, but the best part is we made them together.

MATERIALS

¼ cup meringue powder

½ cup lukewarm water

1 pound powdered sugar, sifted

Gel food coloring

Piping bags

INSTRUCTIONS

1. In the bowl of a stand mixer, combine the meringue powder and water. Using a whisk attachment, mix until frothy. Scrape down sides of bowl to incorporate all the powder into mixture.

2. Add sifted powdered sugar and whip together on medium speed for about 3 minutes. Again, scrape down the sides of the bowl.

3. For piping consistency, whip the icing until soft peaks form and the icing stays in place when piped on cookie.

4. Separate base icing into small bowls (reserve some to adjust consistency levels) and add food coloring until the icing reaches your desired hues. Fill piping bags and outline cookies.

5. To fill in the outlines, create flood icing by adding one to two drops of water to the piping bag at a time. If the icing becomes too thin, add piping icing to thicken it back up to the desired consistency. Fill in outlined designs on cookies.

BY ERIKA YUNG

THE SPREAD LOVE
PROJECT

When my eldest daughter was five years old, I wanted to involve her in a service project. Around that time, I happened upon an amazing artist who painted rocks, wrote messages on them, and left them in places for people to find. I thought it was such a neat idea that we decided to do the same.

We had so much fun painting rocks and thinking of nice things to write that could cheer up someone. Then we went to various places around town and covertly placed them in spots for people to find.

After that first year, it became a tradition of ours for Valentine's Day. We have done the project with materials other than rocks as well, such as tree slices and pinecones.

We tend to keep our pieces on the simple side, but you can get as detailed as you want with this project. If you're doing it with children, however, let them lead the way. Provide some parameters and decide on an overall theme. Then let them create!

It's incredibly important to teach our children the impact they can have on someone's day and possibly someone's life—in both big and small ways. This project is, of course, a small way, but it can still have an impact. Don't underestimate the power of a smile, an encouraging word, a compliment, a hug, or a painted rock. Just do it. Say it. Give it. Spread the love.

MATERIALS

Rocks

Acrylic paints and paintbrush

Optional: Sharpie or paint pen

Optional: sealant

INSTRUCTIONS

1. Find rocks (or buy some from a local craft store if need be). Ideally, you want smooth rocks with a large enough surface for painting and writing.

2. Paint the rocks with acrylic paint and let them dry, then write with a Sharpie or paint over that layer. Or you can just use paint pens for the whole project. We've tried a variety of techniques over the years.

3. We have never sealed the pieces, but that is something that you could do as well with something like DuraClear Gloss Varnish or Krylon UV-Resistant Clear Acrylic Coating. Don't forget to be adventurous and take it beyond rocks as well. The creative possibilities are endless.

BY JILLIAN RAGSDALE

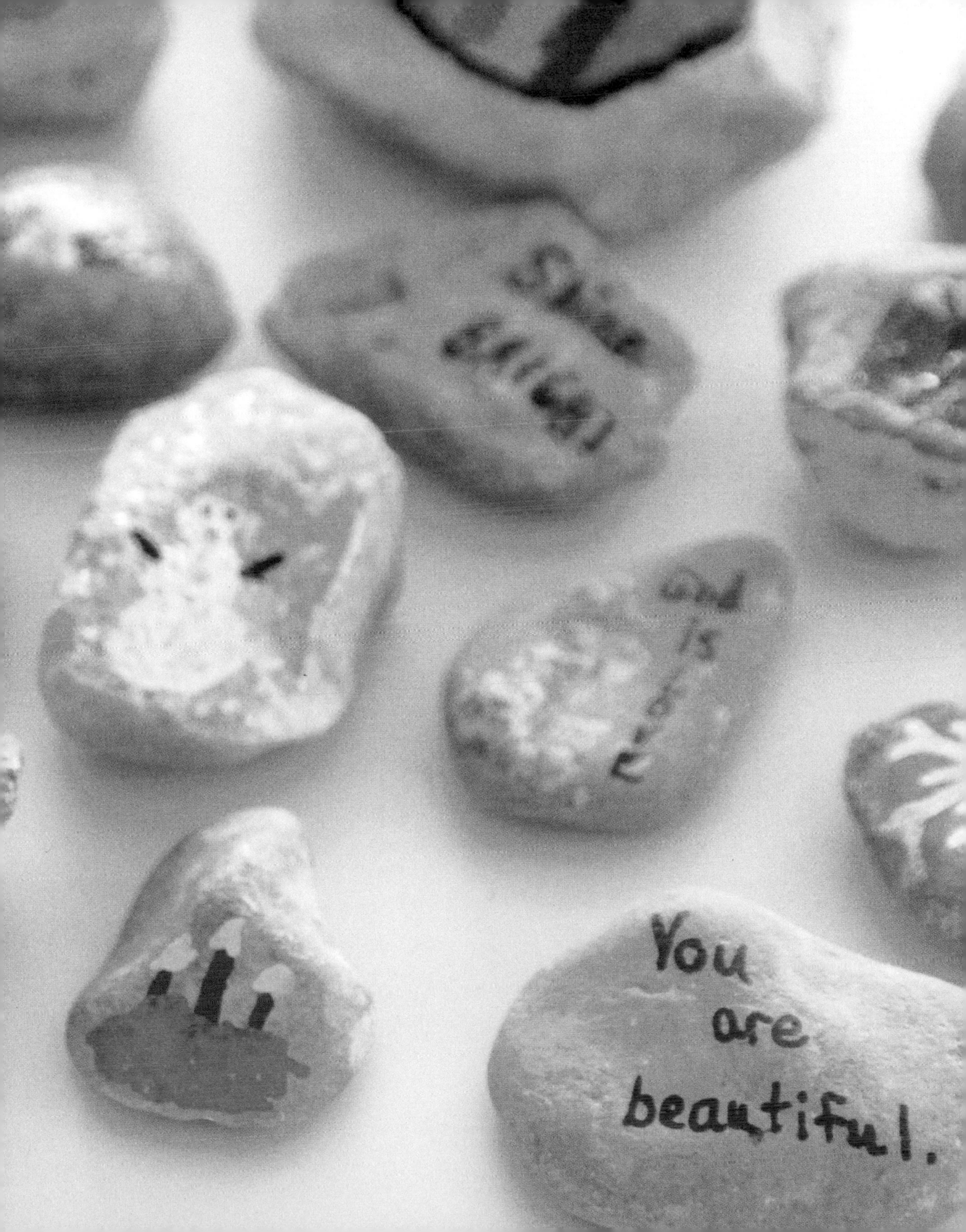
You are beautiful.

RESOURCES AND MATERIALS

Before beginning a handcraft project, always look at the materials list to make sure you have the necessary supplies. The majority of materials can be found at almost any local craft store.

As you delve into the world of handcrafts, you will notice that certain materials and supplies are used frequently, and you might want to begin building your own handcraft supply cabinet. Here are useful items to keep on hand:

- Twine
- Wool roving
- Craft glue
- Hot glue gun
- Scissors
- Wood burner
- Small saw
- Hand drill
- 240-grit sandpaper

- Yarn
- Fabric scraps
- Burlap
- 6-inch or 7-inch embroidery hoop
- Embroidery floss
- Tapestry needles*
- Cross-stitch needles*
- Knitting needles*

- Felting needles**
- Beeswax
- Watercolor paints
- Wooden beads
- Washable tempura paint
- Scraps of ribbon and other adornments

* These needles are usually dull, but always inspect before allowing children to use.

** Felting needles are sharp, so should be used with adult supervision.

CONTRIBUTORS

ABBY MEDAWAR is an energetic mother to four sweet children and is blissfully married to her husband. They live in Grand Rapids, Michigan, where they own and operate a family business in fine jewelry. Their time is spent reading good books, exploring in nature, enjoying a variety of ethnic foods, and serving the church and their community.

AINSLEY ARMENT is the founder of Wild + Free, host of the weekly *Wild + Free* podcast, and author of *The Call of the Wild + Free* and *Wild + Free Handcrafts*. She and her husband, Ben, are founders of the Wild + Free Farm Village and are raising their five children, Wyatt, Dylan, Cody, Annie, and Millie, in Virginia Beach, Virginia. | @ainsl3y

ALISHA MILLER is raising her own little women: four daughters, ages eight and under. Alisha follows the Charlotte Mason method and is thankful for the opportunity to give her children a beautiful and rich childhood. She also is thankful for the journey of life—a journey of learning, loving, and becoming. | @littlewomenfarmhouse

AMANDA GREGG is a transplant from Georgia to Texas, where she lives with her husband and two very silly little girls. Amanda's idea of a good day includes soaking up the sun, lots of laughter, delicious food, amazing music, and a good book. | @amandamillergregg

CAROL ANN SARTELL lives on a small homestead in the Piney Woods region of Texas. Her husband is a police officer and a captain in the Texas Army National Guard. She has three small children, fifteen chickens, two dogs, and a luscious vegetable garden. She is a former public school teacher turned homeschool mama. | @farmish_life

CORY WILLIAMS is a natural-light photographer based out of Chester County, Pennsylvania. She has fallen in love with capturing sweet moments and memories for others. It brings her joy to see and create beauty in the people and spaces around her.
| @cory_williamsphotography

CHELSEA HOLLAND is a wife and mother of five who believes that anything is possible. She loves to learn, no matter what it may be, and has severe wanderlust, longing to see the world. She is a quiet and semi-introverted individual who loves her friends and family. Motherhood suits her.
| @chels_holland

CYNTHIA GARCIA is married to her best friend and has a teenage son whom she homeschools, along with her sister's four kids. Their lives are filled with adventure, learning together, and taking one day at a time. | @garcia3cynthia

ELLE CELAYA is a former public school teacher, now a home-educating mother of three. She is passionate about cultivating creativity in her home through nature study, making art, and providing a living education. She resides by the beach in North County, San Diego, and enjoys exploring the coastlines and mountains. | @wovenchildhood

ERIKA YUNG and her husband raise their two daughters in beautiful San Francisco. After a fun and rewarding career in fashion, she now has the privilege of staying home, nurturing her kids, and pouring love, grace, and beauty into them. | @erikasjoy

HANNAH MAYO lives in South Florida with her husband and four children. She is a writer and photographer who believes in the power of storytelling. When she can find a snippet of free time, she is likely to be found reading, watercolor painting, or enjoying nature. | @hmayophoto

HANNAH WESTBELD is an accidental homeschooler. She was homeschooled growing up but didn't necessarily want to replicate that with her children. She began reluctantly but quickly fell in love with homeschooling. She treasures the time spent with her children, who have truly become her dearest friends. | @myheartshomestead

HEIDI EITREIM is currently a stay-at-home homeschool mom, in her fifth year. She has a BA in art with an emphasis in graphic design and recently reignited her passion for drawing and illustrating when she started teaching her children how to keep a nature journal. | @withheidijoy

JAMIE WOLMA can be found well into the afternoon, still in her jammies, hair in a bun, on the playroom floor with her kiddos reading books or building towers, doing her very best to inspire them to live creatively, intentionally, and passionately. | @mrs.jamie_

JILLIAN RAGSDALE, her husband, and two girls live a joy-filled and adventure-seeking life in the Dallas-Fort Worth area, where they try to spend as much time outdoors as possible. She wants to show her girls how to see and appreciate the beauty everywhere. | @ourgreennest

KATRIEN VAN DEUREN grew up in Belgium but moved to northern Italy when she met her husband, Francesco. Now, almost ten years later, they have twin boys and a baby and make a conscious effort to build a slow, mindful life for themselves in close contact to nature. | @growingwildthings

KIRSTY LARMOUR, her husband, and two daughters were born in four different countries. She is a lifestyle photographer who suffers from extreme wanderlust and is often found documenting the way kids see the world. This usually involves taking lots of photos of her daughters' backs as they adventure through life. | @kirstylarmour

KRISTIN ROGERS loves to laugh, learn, make fun of herself, let her children climb on her, and join them in their homemade forts. Her heart does a "pitter-patter" for nature, adoption, reading, coffee, homeschooling, thrift shops, messy hair, and tattoos. | @kristinrogers

LEA WU is a recovering public school teacher, has homeschooled her two children for four years, and also home-schools three other children. She has a passion for forest hiking and gardening (especially with children) and lives in the beautiful Great Lakes state of Michigan. | @myprojectlivewell

LEAH BODEN is married to Dave; they have four children and live in Coventry, England. Leah has been teaching her children at home for many years inspired by the Charlotte Mason philosophy. She is passionate about empowering and supporting others in their mothering and homeschooling journey. | @modernmissmason

LEAH DAMON was raised on a mission field in the Wolof tribe of the Gambia, West Africa. She and her husband are currently raising and homeschooling their three wild boys in a vintage farmhouse in southeastern Pennsylvania. | @leahdamon

MOLLIE HARDY is a graduate student studying social work, a lifestyle photographer, and wife to a bearded sociology PhD student. Mollie is an advocate for empathy, a believer that vulnerability is a superpower, and a lover of people right where they are. | @mollie_hardy

NAOMI OVANDO lives with her husband and children in sunny Southern California. She homeschools her two boys and little girl and is a hobbyist photographer and loves taking storytelling photos of her family and going on outdoor adventures. | @3bebesmama

NICHOLE HOLZE is an Iowa native now living in the South, happy to claim Arkansas as home. Mama to two incredible adventurers, she is a wanderlust-and-coffee fueled fearless roadtripper who has been known to take off for epic adventures at a moment's notice. | @coleyraeh

RACHEL KOVAC and her husband, Dan, live in south-central Texas with their five children, including their third child who joined their family through international adoption. Rachel seeks out the beauty in everyday moments and is passionate about photography as the medium to document them. | @rachelstitchedtogether

RACHEL ROBINSON has learned so much about who she is behind the camera by showing people a part of themselves they may have forgotten. She is a wild and free momma of three and loves being able to capture this beautiful, crazy life they live. | @rachelrobphotog

SHANNON MOOERS is married to her soulmate and mother to five adventurous children. She enjoys good coffee, slow mornings, the smell of old books, art, and spontaneous road trips. She's game for any adventure that comes her way. Her dream is to sell everything they own and travel when her tribe is grown. | @alwaysroomformooers

SHARON MCKEEMAN is married and has three children that she has homeschooled since the first one was in kindergarten. On her blog she writes honest encouragement for women walking through daily life and grief, and she is completing her memoir on pregnancy loss. She calls sunny Southern California home and loves spending time outdoors with her family. | @sharonmckeeman

SUZI KERN lives in the mountains of East Tennessee with her three children and sleepy old lap dog. She is a regular contributor to the Wild + Free content bundles. | @suziqzikern

ABOUT
WILD + FREE

Wild + Free is a community of families who believe children not only should receive a quality education but also are meant to experience the adventure, freedom, and wonder of childhood. Wild + Free exists to equip families with resources to raise and educate children at home, as well as to encourage and inspire them along the way.

To learn more about Wild + Free and join the community,
visit bewildandfree.org. | @wildandfree.co

CREDITS

Photographs of Pumpkin-Beeswax Harvest Candles craft on pages xii and 3 by Cory Williams. Used with permission. Photographs of Fall Felt Leaf Crown craft on pages 4–7 by Naomi Ovando. Used with permission. Photographs of Pumpkin Cottage craft on pages 8–10 by Elle Celaya. Used with permission. Photographs of Mother Earth Wool Felting on pages 11–18 by Katrien Van Deuren. Used with permission. Photographs of The Thankful Tree craft on pages 19–21 by Abby Medawar. Used with permission. Photograph of "Mothers as Memory Makers" essay on page 23 by Kristin Rogers. Used with permission. Photographs of "Finding the Perfect Tree" Traditions on pages 24–27 by Chelsea Holland. Used with permission. Photographs of A Picture Book Christmas craft on pages 28–31 by Alisha Miller. Used with permission. Photographs of A Celebration of Light craft on pages 32–37 by Rachel Robinson. Used with permission.

Photographs of Winter Table Piece craft on pages 38–41 by Katrien Van Deuren. Used with permission. Photographs of Natural Christmas Tree craft on pages 42–47 by Rachel Kovac. Used with permission. Photographs of Turning Artwork into Festive Decor craft on pages 48–51 by Heidi Eitreim. Used with permission. Photograph of "Collecting Ornaments" Traditions on page 52 by Kirsty Larmour. Used with permission. Photographs of Hand-Embroidered Star craft on pages 54–58 by Abby Medawar. Used with permission. Photographs of How to Draw a Christmas Wreath craft on pages 59–61 by Kristin Rogers. Used with permission. Photographs of Wool-Felted Advent Spiral craft on pages 62–66 by Cory Williams. Used with permission. Photographs of Christmas Garland craft on pages 67–69 by Mollie Hardy. Used with permission. Photograph for "A Mother's Search for Light" essay on pages 70–71 by Hannah Mayo. Used with permission. Photographs of Snowflake Art craft on pages 72–75 by Kristin Rogers. Used with permission. Photographs of "Arroz con Leche" Traditions on pages 76–78 by Cynthia Garcia. Used with permission. Photographs of Nature-Stamped Ornaments craft on pages 79–83 by Naomi Ovando. Used with permission. Photographs of Christmas Cookies as Handcrafts craft on pages 84–87 by Sharon McKeeman. Used with permission. Photographs of "Book Advent" Traditions on pages 88–89 by Jamie Wolma. Used with permission. Photographs of Holiday Crowns craft on pages 90–92 by Suzi Kern. Used with permission. Photographs of Mistletoe Kissing Ball craft on pages 93–95 by Abby Medawar. Used with permission. Photographs of Homemade Advent Calendar craft on pages 96–98 by Kristin Rogers. Used with permission. Photographs of Handmade Wrapping Paper craft on pages 99–101 by Hannah Mayo. Used with permission. Photographs of "The Lion, the Witch, and the Wardrobe" Traditions on pages 102–103 by Hannah Westbeld. Used with permission. Photographs of Storybook Ornaments craft on pages 104–106 by Mollie Hardy. Used with permission. Photographs of Rustic Woven Winter Stars craft on pages 107–112 by Cory Williams. Used with permission. Photographs of Paper Stars craft on pages 113–119 by Rachel Kovac. Used with permission. Photographs of "The Promise of a New Year" essay on pages 120–121 by Katie Okanski. Used with permission. Photographs of Midwinter Lanterns craft on pages 122–127 by Katrien Van Deuren. Used with permission. Photographs of Mindful Love Baskets craft on pages 128–132 by Cory Williams. Used with permission. Photographs of Wildflower Valentines craft on pages 133–137 by Nichole Holze. Used with permission. Photographs of Cupid's Arrow Valentines craft on pages 138–140 by Shannon Mooers. Used with permission. Photographs of Royal Icing Cookies craft on pages 141–143 by Erika Yung. Used with permission. Photographs of The Spread Love Project craft on pages 144–147 by Jillian Ragsdale. Used with permission.

Additional photography credits:

Pages i and x–xi: Alisha Miller

Pages ii–iii: Jamie Wolma

Pages iv–v, vi–vii, 148, and 159: Rachel Kovac

Page viii: Bethany Douglas

Page 150: Mollie Hardy

Pages 151–158: Photographs courtesy of each contributor

Page 160: Katie Okanski

Illustrations:

Recurring trees: pikolorante | Shutterstock

Recurring snowflake for skill-level key: Maria B. Paints | Creative Market

Pages ix, 25 (snow), 36, 50 (snow), 64, 140: everysun | Creative Market

Page 1: Wonderdigi | Creative Market

Pages 5, 9, 29 (books), 73, 108 (acorn), 130: Dainty Doll Art | Creative Market

Pages 9 (wildflowers), 74, 97 (ribbon), 134, 136, 145: Maria B. Paints | Creative Market

Pages 13, 25 (trees), 35 (top greenery), 45 (orange), 50 (deer), 80, 82, 91: Graphic Box | Creative Market

Pages 20, 29 (holly), 35 (berry branch), 39, 55, 60, 68, 69, 85, 94, 105, 106, 108 (branch), 114 (holly): Corner Croft | Creative Market

Pages 86, 92: Paulaparaula | Creative Market

Pages 43, 114 (lantern), 123, 124: Marina Ermakova | Creative Market

Pages 45 (cinnamon stick), 53 (green ornament), 77, 89: By Monash | Creative Market

Pages 49, 97 (scissors), 100 (paintbrush), 149: PaperSphinx | Creative Market

Pages 53 (red and blue ornaments), 100 (sticks): YesFoxy | Creative Market